Monuments of Spanish Wine

LUCENA
A LAS
5,30
GRAN ACONTECIMIENTO TAURIN
6 NOVILLOS-TOROS
DON MANUEL MONTES ACUY
BAEZ EL LIT
GARCIA PALMEÑ
DE LA HABA ZURI
CANO EL PIR
ANTONIO SANCHEZ FUENTE
ANTONIO EL MESIA

Monuments of Spanish Wine

Wim Vanleuven

Photography:
Jaak Van Damme

STICHTING KUNSTBOEK

Introduction

El vino español va bien! We may be sure of that.
The wine history of Spain is a long and proud one. But for the past 15 years, more changes have occurred in it than ever before and anywhere else in the world. New estates were set up and many an appellation was added to the list. The Spanish world of wine was never quite as fascinating as it is now. New generations of wine-producers, many trained in France, others as far away as the USA, took the lead and drastically opted for renewal whilst never letting go of tradition. They are the people who employ the latest techniques and apply them to traditional grape species. And they Spanish wine standards soaring to unprecedented heights. The 'native tang' notion continues to make headway, also with those appellations tending to ignore it in the past (Rioja's e.g.). Rusticity giving way to a more international approach, Spanish wines can truly claim a new label and identity.

This is also why I chose to describe the new wine-producer generation in this book. Some estates can hardly be considered historic. But, owing to the way they manage functioning today, they too belong to the monuments of Spanish wine. And indeed may be considered responsible for Spain's vastly improved standards in the field of wine making. They are the 'young Turcs' determined to impose their way to achieve what they really want: a product with sufficient class and style to rank as a personality in its own right.

Then there are the few large, historically established, estates: they too wanted to participate in the modern generation's evolution and not simply 'rest on their laurels', for they had grasped its significance.

The estates I describe have not been picked by chance. Their selection may nevertheless be an entirely personal one, as it is based on my budding experience in the field. I began my research in 1992, as Spanish wine started to play an important role for me. If the Casero family from La Rioja had not introduced me to Miguel Angel De Gregorio (Finca Allende), this book would probably never have been written. I was also privileged enough to witness Rioja's revival on the spot, and never stopped investigating since.

Then there was Gerard Hernández, lawyer and former colleague of mine who swore he'd convince me the best Spanish wines come from Catalonia's Priorat region. I was a little sceptical at the time. He had nevertheless managed to sufficiently trigger my curiosity: a week later I was pacing down the paths of Priorat's vineyards. A door had definitely opened for me. What Carles Pastrana had me find (and taste) in his Costers del Siurana was the expression of an entirely new Spanish approach, with a passion and determination as never before. I went home a convert.

Much water may have flown under the bridge since; and many by now followed the footsteps of the wine avant-garde. People who so intensely persuaded me of their calling have been pictured in this book. Their story, as much as their wine, shows how deeply they care for their craft and vineyards. Spain went through a similar revolution in the field of gastronomy: Spanish wonder-cooks currently belonging to the culinary arts' 'crème de la crème'. We even reached the point of having a French chef declare a Spanish chef the world's best. No-one would have taken any notice ten years ago!

Nor would we have believed international gastronomy is more than ever associated with Spanish top-class wines. Many young cellarers discovered that wonderful country's possibilities, their reactions in turn, helping me as an author onto the discovery of more 'monuments', always looking further. Johan Sterckx, Belgium's laureate sommelier in 1997, opened many doors for me with his faith in Spanish wine. He too was at the origin of this book. My sincere thanks go also to him.

In the course of all those hesitant first-step years, the greatest encouragement came from my parents. They gave me my original 'love of Spain', doing all they could to facilitate my visits to that fascinating country. It is thanks to them I consider Spain as being my second 'patria' now!

Welcome to the captivating world of Spanish wine! Viewing it will be made easier through Jaak Van Damme's lovely photographs. Spain is more than ever worthy of your attention, as you may soon discover in the pages of this book.
Thank you for letting me try to help document your excellent initiative!

Wim Vanleuven

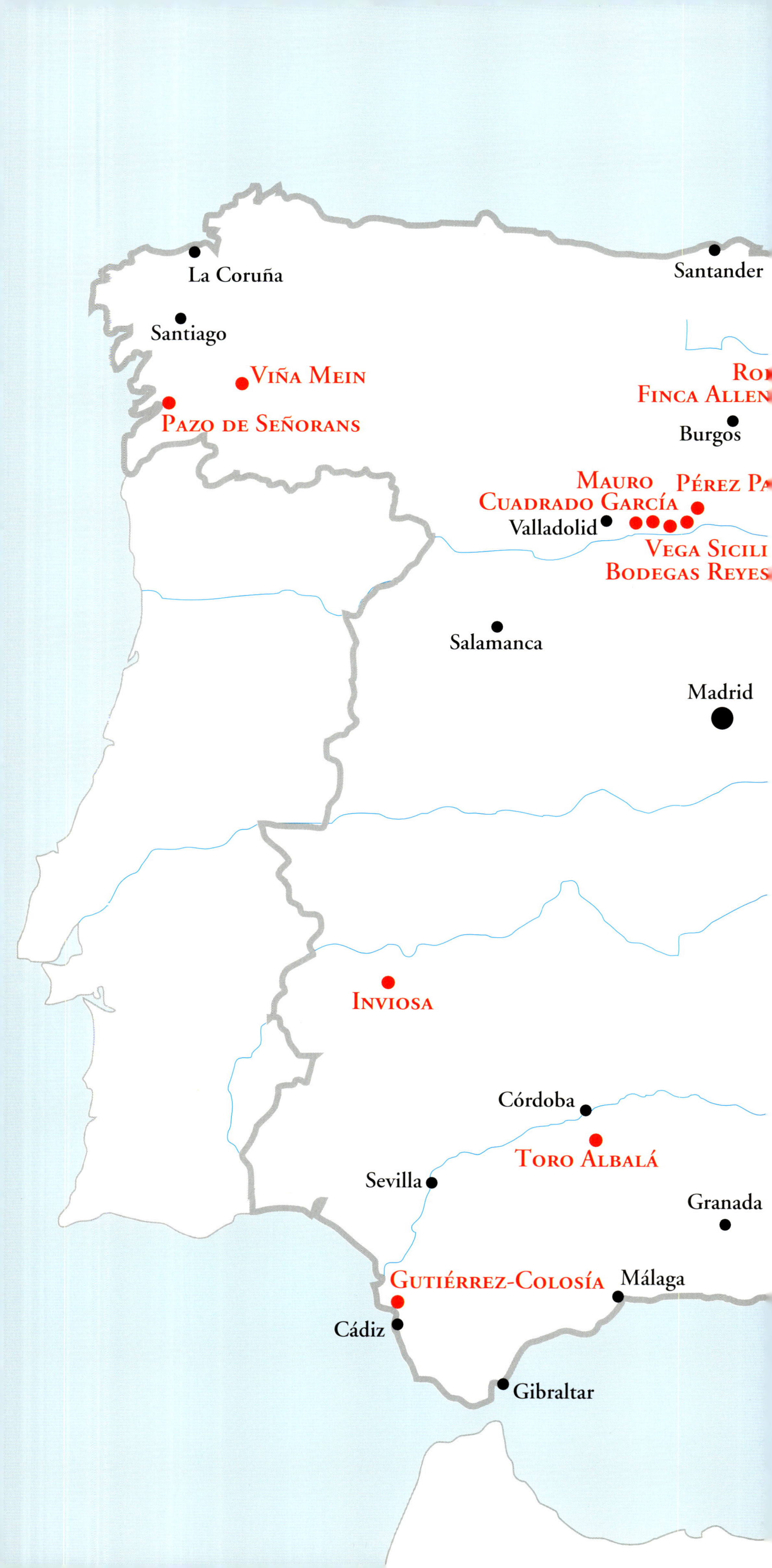
La Coruña
Santander
Santiago
Viña Mein
Pazo de Señorans
Finca Allen
Burgos
Mauro
Pérez Pa
Cuadrado García
Valladolid
Vega Sicili
Bodegas Reyes
Salamanca
Madrid
Inviosa
Córdoba
Toro Albalá
Sevilla
Granada
Gutiérrez-Colosía
Málaga
Cádiz
Gibraltar

an Sebastián
Pamplona
Abel Mendoza
Señorío de Otazu
Artadi
Remírez de Ganuza
Zaragoza
Can Ráfols dels Caus
Puig i Roca
Barcelona
Mas d´en Gil
Albet i Noya
Costers del Siurana
Joan d´Anguera
Bàrbara Forés
Valencia
Alicante
Murcia

Albet i Noya

Can Vendrell
Albet i Noya
08739 Sant Pau d'Ordal
Tel.: 93 899 48 12
Fax: 93 899 49 30

Josep-María Albet i Noya

Owners: Josep-María and Toni Albet i Noya

Oenologists: Marga Torres, Josep-María Albet i Noya

Agronomist: Josep-María Albet i Noya

Surface: 43 ha. in ownership + 80 ha. under supervision

Production: 400,000 bottles

Type:	62%	red
	18%	white
	5%	rosé
	10%	cava

Toni Albet i Noya

The eco-pioneer of Spanish vineyards

The two Albet i Noya brothers covered so much distance within the wine-world they may look back in pride upon the affair. Their bodega is quite recent (it was founded in 1989). The Albet family nevertheless has a thoroughly 'wine-like' history. 'Albet' is not as common as all that a surname in Spain. It has its own specific roots: Josep-Maria and Antoni's forefathers fled the tiny village Albi, in the Tarn district of the Languedoc, in France, during the 13th century. The Albigeois or Cathares, as they were known, were a dissident Christian sect who called themselves 'the good Christians' and claimed purity of faith. They suffered persecution at the hand of Simon de Montfort and the barons of Northern France from 1209. This is also how the Albet family arrived in Spain, where – also fortunately for us, you might say! –, they survived up to this day.

A few centuries later – around 1910 – the brothers' great-grandfather found work in the area of Penedès as a vine-grafting expert. This was quite an important and specialized field at the time: phylloxera had destroyed the larger part of existing vineyards; new vines needed systematic grafting to cross them with the tougher American stock.

On the Sant Pau d'Ordal estate, in a small village between Vilafranca del Penedès and Sant Sadurní d'Anoia, grandfather Albet completed his job to perfection. The land- and vineyard owners were so pleased they asked him to stay on and manage their 210 ha. estate for them. Spain still knew feudal rule in those days – something that would not alter until the end of the 70's – with own harvest still partly needing to be ceded to the landlords.

Fearing for their lives if they tried to stay on in the country, these landowners fled to Barcelona during the Spanish civil war. They never returned. Until 1985, the Albet family lived in the tiny house next to the large empty mansion. The family then decided to put its savings together and acquired the estate. Painstaking restoration and renovation had begun: it may not be over until 2001…

The door is always open at Albet i Noya.

The domain is surrounded by mainly old Macabeu vines, as well as recent plantings of Syrah and Petite Syrah.

Josep-María created his own ecosystem of flowers and herbs in combination with the vines.

The beautiful countryhouse of Can Vendrell.

Sheep are important in providing a natural equilibrium and fertilization.

Josep-María was used to being an early riser; he was only 14 when his father died; by the time he was 16, he went over from his studies to his work and from his work to his studies. Until 1989, all wine-production merely headed for the larger estates. When Josep-Maria started to make a very modest quantity of his own cava, the big houses boycotted him and refused to buy his goods. Which, in the circumstances, they should not have done; for it only strengthened Josep-Maria's resolve…

Tables were drastically turned in 1989. Every Albet penny went into own wine bottling and into researching into 'different', wines. There had been a mere 20,000 bottles in the first year. Their number made history, nevertheless: they happened to contain Spain's first 'ecologically' produced wine. Since then the name and fame of the Albet i Noya eco-wines leapt forward.

The eco-philosophy had not been easy to bring over to own countrymen, in the beginning: no-one was particularly interested; nor indeed were people prepared to buy. Josep-Maria's reaction was typical: without a murmur he sold everything abroad, to anyone welcoming change. The wine turned exclusivity in Spain as a result. With three star restaurants resorting to going all the way abroad to buy Albet I Noya wines! The 'coal' having been taken 'out of Newcastle' you might say! – In the meantime, the wine had covered quite a little ground of its own.

Josep-María estimates all quality wine must automatically be ecologically produced. It stands to reason as a matter of course, in fact: those bodega's not themselves proceeding according to the lines adopted by Albet i Noya are few and far between. Maybe their rules are not quite as rigid; but they too say 'no' to chemical fertilisers, weed killers and pesticides. Most of the remainder bodega's do not avail of the necessary certificates from the body of control to manage true ecology production.

Josep-María checks the arrival of the new 2000 harvest in the cuves.

Albet i Noya wines are more than simply 'ecology': they continue being ahead of their time also in matters of presentation. Josep-Maria could not have been influenced by his father's ways since father never actually bottled any wine very much. There never were too many influences on the part of the 'Spanish style' of the day, fortunately: those were light red wines, quite limp, often left to ripen over a very long time; they tasted stale and oxidized, with an overdose of vanilla. Josep-Maria had always been immensely hungry for new techniques and was prepared to travel anywhere in the world to find out about them. To California and Australia, two countries he had chosen for their stronger wines (with lots of body and structure) and for their use of new French and American oak. 70% of all his own oak today is French.

Josep-María's inquisitiveness and willingness to learn soon had him try out new grape varieties. A major part of the 43 ha. property now harbours different kinds of 'cépages' everywhere. Besides the classics like Cabernet Sauvignon (7 ha.), Tempranillo (5 ha.), Macabeu (4 ha.) en Xarel.lo (5 ha.). Josep-Maria is one of Spain's few to also grow Syrah (6.9 ha.), even Petite Syrah (2 ha.), Arinarnoa (0.4 ha.), Caladoc (0.6 ha.) and Viognier (0.3 ha.).

His research into new, forgotten or disappeared grape-species took him further: all over Spain but also to the Baleares where there still are quite a few pre-phylloxera vineyards. He looked for varieties that were supposed to have died out after the phylloxera, returning with finds. An experimental 1 ha. vineyard was created for 7 'ancient' species. Only 2 were known by their former name. The remainder 5 were given new names. With often no more than one vine (sic!) to represent a species; but enough grafting was done to manage them reproducing. The idea being small scale vinification – at the rate of a few dozen bottles – in 3 or 4 years time, leaving the vines long enough to grow. The operation might also reveal which plants actually belonged to species considered extinct or if they were indeed novelties. The two brothers remaining quite excited at the prospect!

Albet wines from 'normal' vines are every bit as unusual in their own way. Several more Spanish wine-monuments confirm Albet i Noya clearly produces the best Tempranillo in Catalonia. Owing to everyone being jealous of the clone

Cava lies maturing in the old wine cellar.

Josep-Maria's now has in his garden! It was removed everywhere for the past two decades for being 'unproductive'. Quality standards changing, the variety currently sought after most as involving unparalleled quality appears to be that clone's, nevertheless. No more than 10 ha. land or so are known to harbour them. Josep-Maria owns over half.

White 'Albet i Noya'wines are every bit as matchless. The Xarel.lo and the Macabeu vines date back to 1944 and 1950, respectively; they are responsible for several thousands very valuable white wine bottles.

The estate scored high in 1999 with the newly cast Syrah '97, an incredibly seductive and hedonic wine. Only 'mono-varieties' had been produced until 1994: Josep-María tried for a maximum of expression from all his varieties before going over to 'coupages'. He put his first 'Reserva Martí' on the market in 1997, the millésime '94. The wine is an intricate blend of Tempranillo, Cabernet Sauvignon, Syrah, Merlot and Petite Syrah. The wine was named after Martí, Josep-Maria's son, born in 1994 (together with his first 'coupage'!). The amusing label shows two small hands dabbed in red paint or one of Marti's own masterpieces!
More coupages may probably be expected in the future. Was not Adriá born a couple of years ago, Toni Albet i Noya's son?

A characteristic of the brothers being they will never consider anything over and done with, never truly rest 'on their laurels'. They will keep on experimenting and trying out things new. Their activities in more appellation fields are a further proof of this. The Albets' eco-philosophy, in the meanwhile, spreading throughout the vineyards of Spain. A project was started, in Rioja, involving an eco-vineyard in Laguardia (Rioja Alavesa) where eco-Rioja is being produced. In cooperation with Juan-Carlos López de Lacalle of Artadi's – not the least name or reference in the field. The wine will be named Vina Urubi.

The main project remaining the domaine Mas Igneus, in the Priorat region. Josep-María Pujol Busquets from Parxet, in Alella, lent a hand to find the right place in Priorat. Contacts were established with the Poboleda cooperative: some of its members wanted to try out eco-wine production. A small bodega was converted, modern equipment brought in, ancient containers of concrete were used as storage for the French oak barrels. The first wine appeared in 1998: it was a Barranc dels Closos negre 1996, a delightful Priorat of Garnacha, Cariñena and Cabernet Sauvignon. The following year, the Barranc dels Closos also came in its white version, mostly with Garnacha blanca. In 1997, it was the 'FA-series' turn: the FA206, FA112, FA104... Names that are totally incomprehensible to an outsider but hold quite a bit of logic: the abbreviations point to 'élevage': FA indicates a certain type of barrel (Français Allier), the numbering of which is done according to the period of élevage and the age of the barrels (206, two-year old oak for 6 months). In 2000 came the house's top-wine, the 'Costers de Poboleda'. Mas Igneus may certainly be referred to as one of the more successful Priorat's belonging to the 'second wave'. Meanwhile, Anpi Wines was seeing the day. This microscopic enterprise endeavours to import eco-wines from anywhere in the world. It has been making steady progress for more than three years in Spain by now.

Josep-María and Toni take a great deal of pride in their labels: the Col.lecció series, most of all, being particularly special: a different work painted by a young Penedès artist was chosen for each cépage. The painting always representing the estate, viewed from a different angle.

The eco-brothers have a lot in store as yet! Both Josep-María and Toni always play by instinct when it comes to selling their wines, any purely commercial speculation being left out. The wines are distributed by those agents they get on best with, including smaller companies. For the human side stays first and foremost. This is also a reason why, in the Spanish wine world, the brothers are unique and may claim to really stand tall. The consumer may, one day, realise some of Spain's best wines are busy migrating, however. By then it could be too late…

Range

6 red wines

Tempranillo d'Anyada
100% Tempranillo

Lignum negre
Garnacha, Cariñena, Cabernet Sauvignon
6 months on French oak

Col.lecció Tempranillo
100% Tempranillo
12 months on French and American oak.

Col.lecció Cabernet Sauvignon
100% Cabernet Sauvignon
12 months on French and American oak.
Deep red in colour. An intricate nose of black fruit, blackcurrant, cocoa, leather, mint, eucalyptus, the enchanting vanilla scent of young integrated oak. Powerful start off, with strength and refinement showing. Loads of black fruit, wrapped in nicely distributed and well balanced acids.
A terrific finale. A true achievement!

Col.lecció Syrah
100% Syrah
12 months on French and American oak.
Deep red in colour with shades of purple. An explosion of fruitiness in the nose, black forest fruits, bilberries, candied plums, brambe rries, raspberries, blackcurrants, cherries, pleasant whiff of vanilla from nicely dosed oak. Powerful start off, not without its supple tannins: fruit over and over again, à volonté. A seductive body, – fitted with ears and trotters! Brilliant finale. A pleasurable wine.

Reserva Martí
Tempranillo, Cabernet Sauvignon, Merlot, Syrah, Petite Syrah
12 months on new French oak.
Dark red in colour. Sophisticated nose opening up on airing. Minerals, forest fruits, touches of leather, liquorice, coffee, cocoa, green paprika, herbs, black plums. A note of strength combined with daintiness in the mouth. Exquisite balance of acids and tannins that are lithe but make their presence felt. An abundance of fruit. Very extensive finale. Sophistication and class.

5 white wines

Xarel.lo d'Anyada
90% Xarel.lo and 10% other varieties, depending on the year.

Lignum blanc
50% Chardonnay, 50% Sauvignon blanc
3 months French oak.

Col.lecció Macabeu
100% Macabeu
4 to 5 months French oak.
A bright ('Macabeechy')Macabeu gown, touches of roasted nuts in the nose, exotic fruits, peaches, melons and some spicy aniseed hints. A thoroughly fully structured palate with lots of reservations on the side. Pleasant acids and a layering of wood keeping one another in check. Strong and extensive finale.

Col.lecció Chardonnay
100% Chardonnay
4 to 5 months French oak.

Col.lecció Xarel.lo
100% Xarel.lo
4 to 6 months French oak.
Spicy nose with some hints of aniseed and fresh vegetables with a latent florid undertone. A powerful start off in the mouth, wood nicely woven into the fruit. An infrastructure of fine acids. Long and splendid aftertaste with a definite native tang.

1 rosé wine

Pinot Noir/Merlot d'Anyada
50% Pinot Noir, 50% Merlot

5 'méthode traditionnelle'

Cava Brut Reserva
Macabeu, Xarel.lo, Parellada, Chardonnay
18 months 'sur lattes'
A condensed and pure example of a Catalan cava: nose and palate are gooseberry and green apple freshness with a spicy touch to end up with. A pretty and delicate sparkle. Fairly dry owing to the lack of dosage, but sufficiently rounded thanks to lots of fruit (apple, pear, greengage and gooseberry). Pleasant aftertaste.

Cava Brut Nature
Macabeu, Xarel.lo, Parellada, Chardonnay
18 months 'sur lattes'

Cava Brut rosat
60% Pinot Noir, 40% Merlot
18 months 'sur lattes'

Cava Brut Reserva 21 barrica
60% Chardonnay, 40% Pinot Noir
24 months 'sur lattes'.
Chardonnay fermentation on new French oak.

Cava Brut Reserva 21
75% Chardonnay, 20% Parellada, 5% Xarel.lo
24 months 'sur lattes'
Top cava. Pretty bubbles of intense yellow. Pleasant native tang nose with exotic fruit. Gooseberries, apples, pears, more native tang, nicely spicy. Full-bodied palate with well balanced acids and fruits. Sophisticated dosage. A perfect example of both refinement and the expression of native tang. Spiced finale.

Export

80% is destined to the foreign market. Particularly Switzerland, the USA, Britain, Germany, Benelux, Japan, Canada.

ALBET i NOYA
RESERVA
martí
1996
PENEDÈS
Denominació d'origen
SUBIRATS
PRODUCT OF SPAIN

Cellers Puig i Roca

Crta. de Sant Vicenç s/n
Puig i Roca
Les Deveses
43700 El Vendrell
Tel.: 977 66 69 10
Fax: 977 66 65 90

Joan Roca

Owners: Joan Roca and associates

Manager: Joan Roca Amat

Oenologist: Enric Roca Albet

Agronomist: Joan Roca Amat

Area: 20 ha., of which 10 ha. is privately owned.

Production: 150,000 bottles

Type: 50% red
25% white
25% rosé

Barrels of Vinagre agri-dulce lie maturing in various stone huts spread across the domain.

A château in the Penedès

The Mediterranean glistens in the distance. The panoramic view from the Puig i Roca vineyards is simply breathtaking. Here is 'Les Deveses' a place situated in the small town of St. Vicenç de Calders where Joan Roca and Josep Puig were destined to make history.
Both knew each other well before the Puig i Roca adventure. Both Josep Puig and Joan Roca had lived for many years in Chili. Joan Roca orginally comes from a family of wine-growers, and has only known vineyards all his life. For many years he was active in the vineyards in Chili and was involved in selling corks. He returned to Spain at the beginning of the 80s in order to take on an even greater challenge: founding his own bodega.
Josep Puig is a gastronomy man. He spent years cooking for a restaurant in Catalonia, after which he started work as a wine seller in the well-known Torres wine-house. He was involved in establishing Torres in Chili, where he remained for the first five years. Finally he returned to Spain and became export director for Torres. In this position he travelled the world and came into contact with the top of the gastronomic world.
Both Josep and Joan owned a small part of a vineyard in 'Les Deveses'. They decided to join forces and founded 'Cellers Puig i Roca'. New vines were planted between 1982 and 1987, mainly Chardonnay (amounting to 7 ha.) and Cabernet Sauvignon (amounting to 9 ha.) and to a lesser extent Merlot and Cabernet Franc. Initially the total area came to a mere 10 ha. In 1989 the bodega proper was built, and in 1990, after experimenting for a number of years, the first wine, the Augustus Chardonnay was vinified.
The name 'Augustus' was chosen: on the domain are the remains of what was once the Roman Via Augusta… This runs from the south of Spain (Cádiz) to Rome. A few kilometres before this, in Torredembara, is the well-known Arco de Barà which is a well preserved triumphal arch.
The situation was also ideal for making a 'château wine'. The idea of using vineyards around the domain was fairly original in Spain. Most bodegas bought grapes from wine-growers and used it to make their wine. At Puig i Roca the whole process – from planting to bottling – was checked on the domain itself. Indeed, together with Can Ráfols dels Caus they were the pioneers in the Penedès with this château concept.

From 1991 Enric Roca joined 'Puig i Roca' as an oenologist. Enric is Joan Roca's cousin and he too has roots in winegrowing.
The team formed by these three people would make 'Augustus' what it is today: one of the most prestigious wine-houses in Catalonia. This prestige is due mainly to… the grape pickers. Indeed, the customers were the grape pickers. Josep Puig had a great many friends in the world of top gastronomy both at home and abroad and they would come to gather the harvest. Of course this ensured that the Augustus wines would be given a prominent position in the world of top gastronomy. What had started out as a joke soon became a tradition. For the most recent harvests the pickers were accompanied by their wives and children, with the families being served whole banquets. This made the harvesting even more pleasurable…

The same applies to the 'Forum'. A number of barriques of wine vinegar were made for private use from Cabernet Sauvignon. This did not simply involve ordinary wine vinegar but an agri-dulce, which is a slightly sour vinegar that is suitable for use in all sorts of gastronomic dishes. A few customers ordered a number of bottles. This became so successful that it was finally decided to commercialise this 'Vinagre Agri-dulce' under the name of 'Forum'. Soon a white wine vinegar made from Chardonnay appeared on the market. At present Forum is responsible for half of the Puig i Roca sales. Indeed these products are used in higher gastronomic circles all over the world. It has even become a tradition for Forum to be served as part of the annual menu at the presentation of the Nobel prizes.
Josep Puig left the bodega in 1998 to devote himself to a new project in Priorat, the Vinedos de Ithaca, together with his daughter Sylvia. Nevertheless the philosophy of quality is still being continued by the tandem of Joan and Enric Roca.
This philosophy of quality can easily be summarised: approach everything in the very best possible way, without worrying about the quantity. Little more than 36,000 bottles of the best-known wine of the house, the Chardonnay, are still being made in spite of a far greater market demand.
This Chardonnay is usually harvested very early – indeed half way through August it has already reached a level of 13.5% alcohol. Less than 50% of the must is used for the wine which gets its fermentation on new Nevers oak vats. The wine then gets another élevage sur lies for a period of 4 to 6 months, depending on the year. The use of wood is

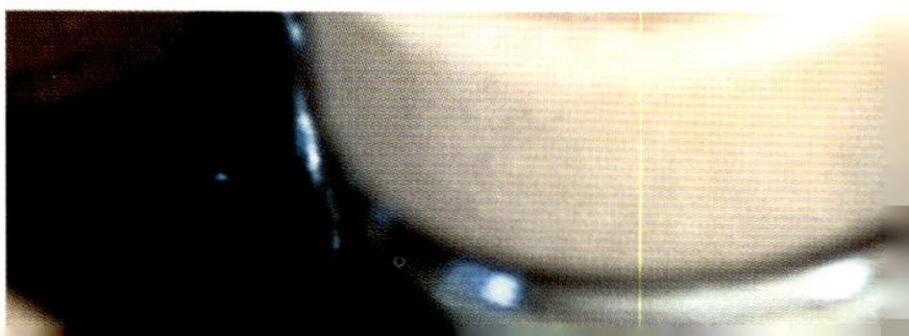

A slightly sour wine vinegar, the Forum is a gastronomic top product and at present accounts for half the domain's turnover.

Typically Catalan pine-trees border the road that runs around the Puig i Roca domain.

Puig i Roca's Roman roots: running through the domain are the remains of what used to be the Via Augusta.

carefully monitored. Enric is very careful about this and watches over the wines as if they were his own children. The 'Californian' style, or highly alcoholic wines with a lot of new oak is easy to imitate in the warm Spanish climate. Indeed, too many fashionable Spanish Chardonnays are guilty of imitating this style. This is not at all the case with Augustus. Here the strength and fruitiness are coupled with elegance and finesse.

Yet another success story of this domain is the rosé. This wine is made from almost 100% Cabernet Sauvignon (for technical reasons the '99 was supposed to contain 10% Merlot). It is a *rosé de saignée* with a short macération pelliculaire. The result is spectacular for a rosé. It is also a rosé that is often used in gastronomy. Enric makes about 30 to 40 thousand bottles of this rosé each year. Once again we get the same story: there is far more demand than supply. The domain also bottles a small quantity of red wines which have undergone a considerable change in style in recent years. The vines are now already 10 years older than in the beginning. The red wines, a Merlot and a Cabernet Sauvignon have a limited élevage on French oak (the second year oak of the Chardonnay), The Cabernet Sauvignon has almost 9 months and the Merlot between 3 to 4 months. The result: wines that are forceful and yet fruity, and have body and are also smooth. In addition to this a limited quantity of Cabernet Franc is made and there is also a top red wine in the pipeline. This reserva should appear at the end of 2001.

The production of these wines will not increase because Enric and Joan only want to use grapes that come from their own vineyards. A good philosophy that will ensure a great future for the domain.

Range

3 red wines

Augustus Cabernet Sauvignon
85% Cabernet Sauvignon, 15% Merlot
9 months 2nd and 3rd year French oak
Dark Red in colour. Typically warm Cabernet nose. Black fruit, leather, mint. Cocoa, spicy hints. Pleasant onset, with beautiful fruit, balanced wood and tannins. Lovely aftertaste.

Augustus Merlot
85% Merlot, 15% Cabernet Sauvignon
3.5 months on 2nd year French oak
Very dark in colour. Complex gamma of forest fruits in the nose, ripe and preserved fruits, with a whiff of wood. Elegant structure in the mouth, especially the abundant black fruit that comes to the fore. Juicy. Sexy finale.

Augustus Cabernet Franc
100% Cabernet Franc
3.5 months on 2nd year French oak
Dark red in colour. Typical Cabernet Franc nose, ripe fruit, green paprika, spicy tones, black olives. Smooth onset, with a little reserve in the midriff – strong tannins that are nevertheless smooth. Ripe finale. Good aftertaste.

rosé wine

Augustus Cabernet Sauvignon rosé
90% Cabernet Sauvignon, 10% Merlot
A Rosé wine with plenty of colour. In the nose an intense bouquet of violets, raspberries and other red fruit, cherries, coffee beans, red paprika. A lot of fraîcheur in the mouth and yet with sufficient body. Long aftertaste for a rosé. A good full wine.

white wine

Augustus Chardonnay
100% Chardonnay
4.5 months on new French oak
Clear yellow colour. Complex nose of tropical fruit, touches of butter, toast, melon, honey. Full in the mouth with lovely acids and the emergence of fruit especially. Perfect balance between wood and wine. Very good acids present. Impressive finale. A great wine.

other products

Forum, Vinagre agri-dulce de Cabernet Sauvignon

Forum, Vinagre agri-dulce de Chardonnay

Flavius, Vinagre agri-dulce de Cabernet Sauvignon Reserva

Export

60% of the production, mainly Australia, Benelux, Germany, Great Britain, Japan, USA, Switzerland.

AVGVSTVS
EMBOTELLADO
1999
EN LA PROPIEDAD
AVGVSTVS
Chardonnay
PENEDÈS
Denominación de Origen
Alc. 13% vol
75 cl.
CELLERS PUIG & ROCA, S.A. - EL VENDRELL-ESPAÑA
R.E. 6868-T

Can Ràfols dels Caus

08739 Avinyonet del Penedès
CAN RÀFOLS DELS CAUS
Tel.: 93 897 00 13
Fax: 93 897 03 70
E-mail: canrafols@seker.es

Carlos Esteva

Owner: Carlos Esteva

Oenologists: Carlos Esteva and Jordi Cantí

Agronomist: Ferran Peral

Surface: 450 ha., including 50 ha. vineyards

Production: 315,000 bottles

Type: 37.9% red wine
29.36% white wine
22.3% rosé
10.31% cava

View of Can Ràfols dels Caus that covers an area of 500 ha.

Wine, art and culture in harmony

Carlos Esteva, the owner of this estate, is a real epicurian. He comes from a good family and completed his studies as an economist in Barcelona. He first went into the family business for a while but eventually decided to leave everything behind for Menorca, in 1973.
There, he just 'lived', enjoying life to the full. For his income, he took on house-restoration: Menorca has many little tumble-down dwellings. Carlos liked art and architecture and he could 'go wild' in Menorca! It was pure bliss. Time passed. After some six years however, he suddenly remembered he also had a family estate in Penedès...
In 1979 he returned to the mainland and elected domicile in Can Ràfols dels Caus. The estate is located in Avinyonet del Penedès. Geographically, it belongs to the Garràf, the stony rock-formation coast South of Barcelona. With his brothers, he had inherited the estate; he decided it would live there from now on, and started the project of a lifetime: Can Ràfols dels Caus.
The history of the estate goes far back in time; Carlos Esteva could not really find any detailed accounts of it, the old documents having been destroyed in a fire during the Spanish civil war in the 30's.
One thing is certain: the date that has been engraved on the house itself is 1634 and it had long belonged to the Ràfols family. The estate being in a cliff-area, its grounds were mainly destined to planting vineyards. The more fertile inland soil were mostly kept to grow grain. But the estate was also large and had some of the area's best exploitation possibilities. The estate was acquired by the Esteva's during 1940, or by Carlos' grandfather, Jacinto Esteva. Both the grandfather and the father usually resided in Barcelona, however. The estate's house slowly sank into oblivion and ruin.
The state of affairs did not greatly worry Carlos, a fervent admirer of the architecture of the past and used as he was to restoring huge mansions. He started renovation works in 1979 and proceeded bit by bit. The enterprise bore fruit: the house is, without doubt, the best renovated masía in Catalan countryside. It now harbours the bodega's offices, Carlos' own apartments and the bodega itself with all its vinification halls.

Carlos' plan, when enthusiastically starting the operation in 1979, had been to mainly produce top quality wines on the estate, native tang included and based on the principle of 'don't count the cost'. The project would only pay for itself in the longer term; but he took on the challenge anyway.

Until 1979 wine, mostly in bulk, was sold to the big producers in the area. Mainly white wine of the classic Penedès varieties, like Macabeu, Xarel.lo and Parellada. Red grapes were planted too, if few in number: Tempranillo, Cariñena and Sumoll. Then there were some splendid orchards with peach- and apple trees – total production amounted to some 90,000 l. wine in all.

First, the bodega section was fully restored and modern equipment brought in for the making of quality-wine. For a newcomer to Penedès such an approach was considered

House and bodega: painstakingly renovated by their owner.

Carlos Esteva has managed to evoke the atmosphere of former times once more, right down to the very last detail.

revolutionary at the time: most people continued to produce wine the old-fashioned way and selling it to the big wine and cava companies.

Virtual treasures in the way of old vines had been waiting for Carlos at the estate: the Xarel.lo, Macabeu and Parellada, planted in between 1945 en 1962. But Carlos wanted more. In 1980, he planted his first new species: 1700 Chenin blanc (Spain's first) and 700 Xarel.lo vines. In spite of disapproval, Carlos made up his mind to work with red grapes, adding a few vines of those. In 1979 he found a mere 3100 Tempranillo vines, the kind that had been planted in 1972. From 1981 onwards, he added all he could to the region' established species: over 3000 Merlot + another 1000 Tempranillo's. He stayed consistent over he years, continuing to build up stocks on the different soils and parts of his vast 450 ha. estate. So much so he exceeds the 50 ha. today! He was the region's pioneer for many a grape-species: the Merlot, followed by the indispensable Cabernet Sauvignon, the Cabernet Franc, the Pinot Noir, the Syrah, the Monastrell, not forgetting the Arinarnoa, Caladoc, Nebbiolo, Portan and Graciano. In the white variety he also planted Chardonnay, Moscatell, Sauvignon blanc, Incroccio Manzoni, Macabeu, Chenanson and Roussane.

His first red wine was put on the market in 1984. The older barrels were still in chestnut wood, at first. In fact, very little wood was resorted to, Carlos believing most of all in bottle ripening. Even today, in comparison to his colleagues in the area, he has very little ripening on wood. The reason for the bottle ripening option being Carlos aims most of all for balance in his wines.

The 2 last series, red, white and rosé, were the Petit Caus wines and the Gran Caus wines. The first always coming from younger vines, to drink young, with a mighty fruit bouquet; the others from the older vines receiving a limited layering on wood – excluding the Gran

Carlos is a keen art collector and has many works by young, mainly Catalan artists in his home.

Caus blanco and the Gran Caus rosado. The structure of the Gran Caus wines also predisposed to their storage and keeping.
Carlos took on yet another challenge after a while: 'Caus Lubis'. The wine, made from 100% Merlot, is famous since then for being the best Merlot in Spain. Merlot mainly originates in 'Cervell de Gat' soil('Cerebro de Gato' or 'cat's brains' in Spanish), a slightly sinister description for substrata of clay mixed with fragments of solidified chalk, making it look like brains. Another project currently in the lift appears to be the 'Ad Fines', a 100% Pinot Noir. Like many wine-producers outside Bourgogne, Carlos Esteva wanted to try out this stubborn and rebellious grape. The result will be on the market soon. Besides 2 more novelties for 2000: two white toppers, unique in Spain: the 'Vinya La Calma', made out of 100% Chenin blanc and the 'Vinya el Rocallís', made out of 100% Incroccio Manzoni. A grape species to raise a few eyebrows amongst seasoned wine-freaks. Incroccio Manzoni is an Italian cross of Riesling and Pinot blanc. Results are flabbergasting. Both wines are called after the vineyards that produced them. 'La Calma' is on mainly eroded land with a great deal of chalk and much fossilized matter. Its soil is very light and fine, conferring much fraîcheur and elegance. 'El Rocallís' has a similar subsoil with more clay elements added. Hence the slightly oilier feel of the wine.
Weed killers and insecticides are out; none of Spain's large estates resorting to them very much anyway. A mere 25% of all vineyards is planted the traditional 'en vaso' way (en gobelet). The remainder is mostly 'en espaldera' (en guyot). The vines climbing to a fair height to capt as much sunlight as possible on the leaves.
Carlos is one of the few Spanish wine-producers to be a member of the 'Académie Internationale du Vin', an association gathering the most prestigious wine names in its midst. He also believes that drinking a good wine tells you a lot about the person who made it!

Carlos' wines do distinguish themselves through their sophistication and refinement. They are also true 'vins de terroir' made in Catalonia. Practically works of art. It speaks to reason when you know Carlos is a keen art collector: many a young artist's canvas is displayed in the masía. Another example of his faith in art are is wine labels! Carlos Esteva is clearly one of Penedès' pioneers. With his wines but also in his approach. Someone who has a tale to tell, a large part of which is left untold as yet.

A colourful range of different varieties has been planted on this domain, including some that are quite new to Spain.

The terroir on the Can Ràfols dels Caus is exceptional. There are many lime particles and fossils in the sand, clay and rocky soil. The 'Vinya La Calma'.

Range

4 red wines

Petit Caus tinto
Cabernet Franc, Merlot, Tempranillo, Syrah, Monastrell

Gran Caus tinto
Cabernet Sauvignon, Cabernet Franc, Merlot
12 months on French oak, including 20% new
Dark red and clear when poured out. Nicely evolving nose of red fruit, cocoa, leather, delicate wood and minerals. Followed by black liquorice and the Cabernet franc surfacing also later, green paprika, gooseberry and mint. Mouth-filling and fairly strong start off, developing gracefully; fruity with nicely dosed acids. A classic through and through in body and refinement. Beautifully rounded finale.

Caus Lubis
100% Merlot
12 months French oak
Bright red in colour. Mineral nose with very slender and crested shades, delicately interwoven wood and small touches of leather. Very round and balanced palate. Powerful but dosed. Sophisticated red berry overtones. Fine acids. Long finale with a very fine aftertaste. Real class.

Ad Fines
100% Pinot Noir
layering on French oak (7 to 12 months)

4 white wine

Petit Caus
Xarel.lo, Macabeu, Chenin, Chardonnay, Muscat

Gran Caus blanco
Chardonnay, Chenin, Xarel.lo
Shniy yellow straw when poured out. Very fresh and pleasant nose, beautifully herby, a little of the buttery taste of Chardonnay. Resurfacing minerals. Nicely cool start-off, delicate acids in its midriff. Drawing out slightly more fully and mellow towards the end. Sophisticated aftertaste.

Vinya La Calma
100% Chenin blanc
Fermentation on new French oak.
Bright yellow in colour. A very tight nose at first, neutral. After a while: symphony of fragrances, minerals, fennel, fresh herbs; slightly florid with white roses, tangerines, citrus. Nice acidity in the mouth with many layers edging onto mellowness, dominant fresh herbs. Long aftertaste. Very fine and sophisticated. A wine that takes its time.

Vinya El Rocallís
100% Incroccio Manzoni
Fermentation on new French oak.
Bright yellow in colour. Also a very tight nose. Opens up later and comes in a variety of shades: very spicy, but slightly more mellow than the first. More florid touches, grapefruit, peaches, honey and a dash of cinnamon. Plenty of sweet things in its nose, mineral touches towards the end. A delicate but also firm start off. Mellower and a little fatter than the Vigna de la Calma. Overtones of citrus. Nice acids with mineral content. Very extensive and refined aftertaste.

2 rosé wines

Petit Caus rosado
Merlot, Tempranillo, Syrah and Cabernet Franc

Gran Caus rosado
100% Merlot
A deep antique shade of pink on being poured out. A very authentic nose of sweet gum with some herbs and much fruit. Quite a powerful start-off for a rosé. Plenty of movement in the palate: full-bodied and fruity, very nearly a red wine, with tannins and nicely dosed acids. Lingering aftertaste. A very unusual rosé wine.

2 'méthode traditionnelle'

Gran Caus, Cava Brut natural
Xarel.lo, Chardonnay en Macabeu

Gran Caus, Cava Brut natural rosado
100% Pinot Noir

Export

34,5% of all production, mainly Europe, the USA and Japan.

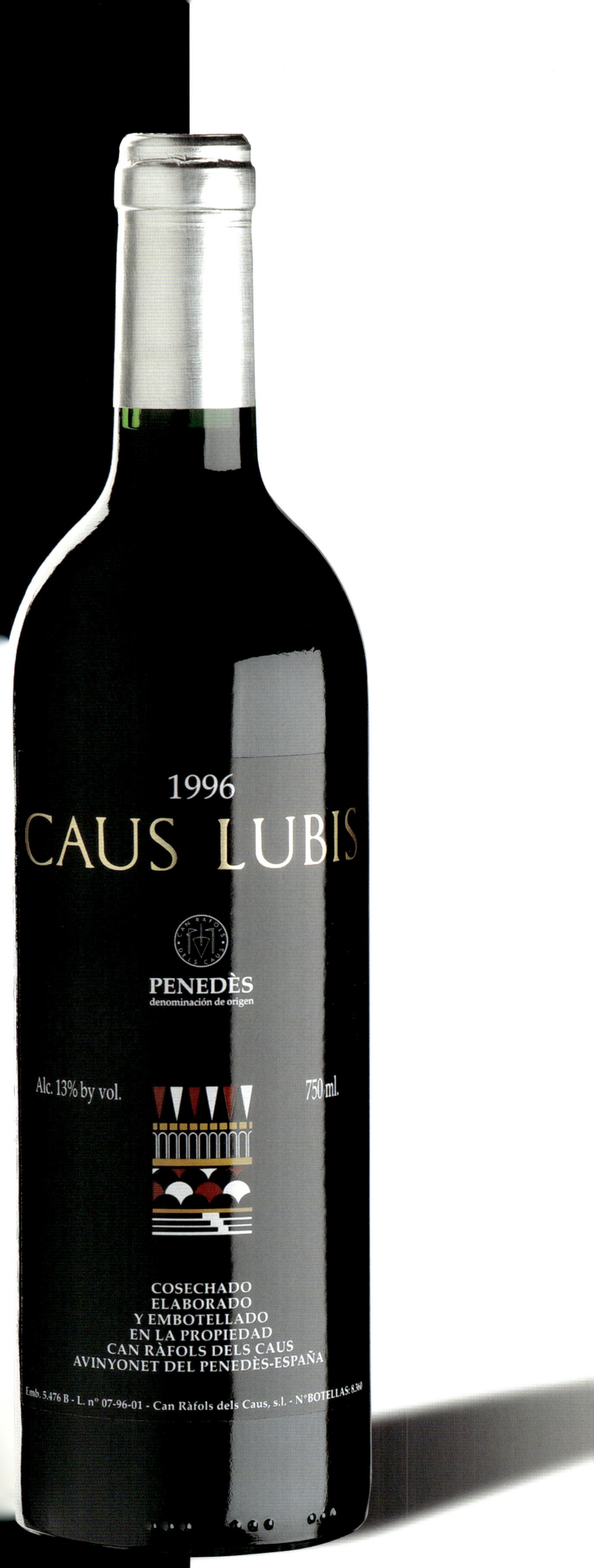
1996
CAUS LUBIS
PENEDÈS
denominación de origen
Alc. 13% by vol.
750 ml.
COSECHADO
ELABORADO
Y EMBOTELLADO
EN LA PROPIEDAD
CAN RÀFOLS DELS CAUS
AVINYONET DEL PENEDÈS-ESPAÑA
Emb. 5.476 B - L. nº 07-96-01 - Can Ràfols dels Caus, s.l. - Nº BOTELLAS: 8.360

Cellers Joan d'Anguera

Major 29
CELLERS JOAN D'ANGUERA
43746 Darmós
Tel.: 977 41 83 48
Fax: 977 41 83 02

The youngest generation: the brothers Josep and Joan Anguera

Owners: Josep and Joan Anguera

Daily guided tour: Mercé Pons Juanpere

Oenologists: Joan, in cooperation with Josep Anguera

Oenologist and agronomist: Josep Anguera, in cooperation with Joan Anguera

Surface: 30 ha. in ownership

Production: 90,000 bottles

Type: red with 60% vino joven and 40% crianza

The 2 brothers are already the 7th generation of Cellers Joan d'Anguera

Two generations, one outlook

Tarragona is more than just a pretty face with an impressive Roman past. It also is Catalonia's main DO! The appellation includes some 83 communes, all from the 3 comarca's: Camp de Tarragona, Priorat and Ribera d'Ebre. There are many villages within the comarca Priorat but not necessarely all belonging to the DO Priorat. Which represents a great deal of difference for them! Anything from within comarca Priorat and Ribera d'Ebre is usually marked on the label, since this represents better quality wine. The additional 'Tarragona-subzona Falset' mention puts the wine in a category of its own, well outside the main Tarragona wine stream.

Differentiating is soon justified: the Falset sub-zone is fast turning into a new DO, the Montsant DO, – named after an imposing mountain range to the back of Falset. To the Joan d'Anguera estate, in the incredibly tiny Darmós village (200 inhabitants), it does not matter a bit. The estate resolutely opting for quality from the start. The trend was confirmed with Josep Anguera Beyme as its manager. Before Josep, any wine that was produced was also quickly, and in one go, sold. Unfortunately, Josep only just recently died and this had some repercussions on the family estate. It exists since 1830 and has a long tradition in wine-making. Josep, a man of the 6th generation, had a different approach: gaining insight into possibilities and looking to the better future of the area. By 1980 he already moved far enough ahead to try out something new: Josep had noticed the soil, most of all in its colour and the characteristics presented by its grit, strongly resembled some Australian soils. The Shiraz vine manages to thrive in Australia. The rock formation, with a strong pink, was unlike Australia's 'Terra Rosa'. This was a very clever observation of his, conclusive in its simplicity: both soil and climate – being a lot of sunshine and the proximity of the sea- were indeed similar; likewise grape-types therefore ought to do well in both these regions. And they do! His Syrah's were revolutionary in Spain at the time he introduced them. Even the Cabernet Sauvignon was considered an exception outside Rioja. Torres, from the Penedès, staying a curiosity in those days.

The Syrah grape was cultivated here for the first time in Spain.

In contrast to the heavy, short-time investment trends displayed by many estates, – involving the manufacture of expensive party wines, made using new vines e.g.... – Josep Anguera never floundered in his search for quality. As long as his Syrah and Cabernet Sauvignon stayed below 20, no top-class wines would be tried out, simply because this was a contradiction in terms!

Josep tended his vines for 20 years and watched them grow. From 1984 to 1996 he only produced young wine, in a 45% Syrah, 35% Garnacha and 20% Cabernet Sauvignon coupage. This gave his fruity young wine lots of body, the short (2 to 3 days) maceration. liberating the full bouquet. He used to bring out an annual 50,000 bottles. He never made another but his talents and discrimination bore fruit: most of the production was rapidly snapped up for export.

Josep waited for his wines to grow every bit as patiently as he watched his own two sons grow. He hated rushing things. His elder son, who is also named Josep, was trained as an agronomic engineer; Josep jr. published a thesis on the 'founding of a wine-estate'. His younger son, Joan, is an oenologist; but much of his practical education came from his father. Both young men also followed a course on storage-wine types in Bordeaux.

The estate is a family estate in the true sense of the word: Josep's widow, Mercedes, assuming its leadership and general management. She used to be head of a secondary school and insists on the same excellence in day-to-day running. Like Josep with his wine-making.

In 1996, the family took another step forward: producing the wine layering on French oak. This is how the ' Finca l'Argatà 1996' came into being. The wine was put on the market in 1998 and turned out an immediate success in Spain and abroad. It is a 40% Syrah, 35% Cabernet Sauvignon, 15% Garnacha and 10% Cariñena. It was given a 12 months ripening on American and French oak. There had been lots of arguments as to which wood to use to best fit in with the wine. Josep sr. opted for American or Bosnian oak. The younger generation -Josep jr. and Joan-went for the French oak. Recent millésimes confirm the younger generation was right, this time! More French oak thus staying used for the latest Finca l'Argatà and 100%

Housed in the 'sweet' treasury of grandfather Anguera are rancio sweet white and red wines, dozens of years old.

View of the Garnacha vines 'en vaso'.

French oak going into the layering of the house's top-wine, the 'El Bugader'.

'El Bugader' was first made in 1998. It will be put on the market towards the end of 2000. Like the Finca l'Argatà, the new wine was named after a vineyard. The estate does not abide by traditional Spanish denominations, 'crianza' and 'reserva', for its wine. Quality counts, naught else. Whether this involves a young wine, a crianza or a reserva.

The oldest Syrah vines are found in the 'El Bugarder' vineyard and yield the best quality wine of all. This wine taking the estate to the level of Spain's truly greats. It is also quite unique, with a coupage of 70% Syrah, 15% Garnacha and 15% Cabernet Sauvignon. The fruit of Spain's best vines goes into the making of this wine.

The wine was the result of Josep Anguera Beyme's 20 year long project, successfuly rounded up by his two sons. Like their father, they have always shown a lot of common sense and are well aware of the time, trouble and investment that are necessary for the making of such a wine. The best proof of their dedication are the vineyards themselves: on pacing along, you will soon recognize those belonging to Cellers Joan d'Anguera, also when a complete stranger to the area. Far more trouble has obviously been taken by the Anguera's!

Half the vineyards (there are some 30 ha. in all) are laid on in the traditional bushy manner ('en vaso' or 'bushvines') , when older Garnacha and Cariñena vines with an average age of

40 most of all. The remainder half is planted in rows ('en espaldera' or 'en guyot'); these involve mainly the Syrah and the Cabernet Sauvignon. A lot of hard work is done each winter; in spring, the 'vendange verte' ('poda en verde') determines what the ideal volume of the leaves must be to obtain the better photo-synthesis and grape-ripening. Only the vino joven is filtered after ripening. Anything ripening on oak does not get filtered. The wine is naturally stabilized by the winter cold.

Also truly special is the 'vi Dolç', a sweet red wine, 100% Garnacha. Its production is restricted: a mere 1,000 bottles every now and then leave the bodega. 1996 was the only millésime so far; many hopeful clients expect it to soon be followed by another. For, if some divine nectar is to be found anywhere, any time: this is it! The strong and sweet red wine tradition is strongly rooted in Tarragona country. The famous 'Tarragona Clásico' stays mostly on oak for a 12 years. It is a curiosity by now: nowhere to be found. The gorgeous delicatessen of Josep jr.'s family cellar go further still: sweet white and red rancio-wines, 20 and 50 years old. A real treasure-throve in other words. But one that is for own consumption: it does not reach the market.

The vines of Cabarnet Sauvignon and Syrah planted
'en espaldera'

The brothers, Josep and Joan, have a number of plans in store for the future. Builder-works were started of late, involving a greater bodega surface and to add facilities for work. Invariably keeping the principles of Josep sr. in mind: care and quality!

The 7th generation is thoroughly worthy of Josep Anguera's visionary approach. The small and exclusive estate belonging to DO Tarragona will undoubtedly assert its status even more, with the creation of the new DO Montsant most of all.

Range

3 red wines

Joan d'Anguera, Vino joven
45% Syrah, 35% Garnacha, 20% Cabernet Sauvignon
This annual wine, on the market towards the midst of November, has a nose with masses of fruit and plenty of sweet things, strawberries and raspberries. Fairly hefty palate nevertheless, with goodly acids and tannins in infrastructure. Nice length in aftertaste for such a young and fruity wine.

Finca l'Argatà
40% Syrah, 35% Cabernet Sauvignon, 15% Garnacha, 10% Cariñena
12 months ripening on French oak and on American oak (new + 2nd + 3rd year)
Intense nose of black fruit and liquorice with delightful vanilla overtones, scalding, some leather and here and there a 'touch of the wild'. Powerful palate but tannins staying lithe. Much body, high fruit content. Lingering aftertaste. Scrumptious and thoroughly hedonic!

El Bugader
70% Syrah, 15% Garnacha, 15% Cabernet Sauvignon
12 months ripening on new French oak
The colour of ink, a very dark mirroring. Nose with a huge amount of fruit (Syrah!), hints of roasted liquorice, scalding. An explosion of all kinds of different flavours in the palate, fruit, acids; vast quantities of tannins but well balanced. Very long aftertaste with a strong end-note.

1 sweet wine

Vi Dolç
100% Garnacha
Wine oscillating between the old rancio-style and the new sweet 'in's'. Very nice nose practically devoid of oxidation. Mainly masses of black fruit, chocolate, cocoa and touches of spicy mint. A sweet-melody palate with a strong acid infrastructure. Endless aftertaste be relishable to the full.

Export

80% of all production is for export, mainly to the U.S.A., Japan, Britain and Switzerland.

El
BUGADER
1·9·9·8
TARRAGONA
Denominación de Origen
ELABORADO, CRIADO
Y EMBOTELLADO EN
LA PROPIEDAD POR
J.ANGUERA BEYME
DARMÓS -TARRAGONA
PRODUCT OF SPAIN
JOAN D'ANGUERA

Mas d'en Gil

43738 Bellmunt del Priorat
Finca Mas d'en Gil
Tel.: 977 83 01 92
Fax: 977 83 01 52

Pere Rovira Rovira

Owner: Pere Rovira Rovira

Oenologist: Toni Coca

Oenologist-agronomist: Josep Vidal

Area: 30 ha. privately owned
and 15 ha. under control

Production: 27.900 bottles

Type: 85% red
15% white

Arbequina-olives

Pere Rovira Rovira's dream

Pere Rovira Rovira is not your typical winegrower. One would expect most farmers to know their own domain – as well as that of the neighbour's – very well. Outside the appellation this is a difficult matter for some. But not for Rovira Rovira. He was born into a family with a tradition of winegrowing in Penedès in Catalonia. However, a Catalan by birth, he was more attracted to the commercial side than to the technical side of the wine industry. From 1962 he travelled all over Spain and became immersed in the wine, alcohol and grape juice industries. He became familiar with every aspect of Spanish geography, and there was not a single vineyard or bodega that he had not visited. No matter what village you come from in Spain, when meeting Rovira Rovira you will always be told: 'Oh and when you get back to your village, give my regards to so and so, who has a vineyard there and there.' Not only did Rovira Rovira get to know his Spanish geography better, he was also able to follow the evolution of wine in different areas from close range. Indeed there is nothing he doesn't know about the style of the wine and the manner in which the work is done in whatever bodega you care to mention.

He devoted most of his time to buying and selling wine. Not per case, but per tank. Rovira Rovira sold mainly bulk wines to supermarkets or wine shops all over the world, always looking for the best quality at the best price. Because of this, not only did he get to know Spain very well, but he travelled all over the world selling millions of litres of Spanish wine. He still remembers quite clearly the way in which people looked at him in countries abroad during the sixties: a look of contempt for a small Spaniard trying to sell his Spanish wines. At that time Spanish wines were often synonymous for primitive concoctions, poorly vinified but very cheap. And so the deal was usually clinched. Today however, things are the other way round: Spanish wines are in demand all over the world and are highly popular in the large-scale distribution industry. Nowadays Rovira Rovira is one of the most important bulk traders of the Iberian peninsula.

Having been born into the wine world. Rovira Rovira actually wanted to do more than simply buy and sell wine. This is why the next step, that of making his own wine, came

Old Garnacha vines at least 50 years old in Bellmunt del Priorat.

The mule is the only winegrowing 'machine' that can reach any part of the vineyards on the domain.

quite naturally. In 1967 he founded a bodega in the Penedès Mas Pujó. Later on, at the end of the seventies, he bought Cavas Hill also situated in the Penedès, together with a friend. Besides small quantities of Penedès wines, mainly Cava was produced.

Rovira Rovira's ambition grew together with the evolution in the Spanish wine landscape. He had also closely followed the revolution in the Priorat appellation. He had admired the success of the Costers del Siurana project, and, in a way that is typical of someone who is passionate about wine, he was determined to also undertake something in the region, certainly after sampling a few of the super terroir wines of the new Priorat generation. And in his own Rovira Rovira manner, he wanted to do this well and not simply blindly invest and plant new vines.

When the Masia Barril domain was put up for sale, he bought it without a moment's hesitation. Masia Barril is a story all on its own, involving one of the classical 19th-century Priorat bodegas owned at that time by the family of the well-known painter and playwright, Santiago Rusinol who was one of the founders of Catalan modernism. In 1931 the domain (of a total of 85 ha.) was bought by Rafael Barril Figueras. Since that time Masia Barril has become a classic of the Priorat wines: together with Scala Dei he was one of the few to bottle his wine (since 1981).

With the advent of the new Priorat wines and the Costers del Siurana project, the style, to put it euphemistically, lagged behind somewhat. The last owner, Rafael Barril Dosset, promoted his wine under the motto of 'a new Priorat in keeping with an old tradition'. In his view, innovation lay in making aromatized wine, with supplements in the vat of herbs taken from the domain. In addition to this they also made the typical rancio, oxidized wines. It was not even fifty years ago that this type of wine was the most important wine style of Catalan. There are all sorts of rumours about the last Masia Barril wines dating

form the middle and end of the 90s, augmented by the fact that the domain and the vines were neglected and have consequently deteriorated.
Just in time (at the beginning of '98), Rovira Rovira decided to buy the domain. At the same time he also bought the adjoining 40 ha. 'Finca del Sas' so that the total area amounted to 125 ha. He rechristened the domain 'Finca Mas d'en Gil', which was the former name of the domain.
The change that took place within the space of barely a few months was spectacular. Rovira Rovira set a team of agriculturalists to work, with the aim of restoring everything as soon as possible. What they found was a wealth of old vines. An unbroken area of 40 ha. of Garnachas and Carinenas that are more than 40 years old is without doubt quite unique in the Priorat. Moreover, 2 ha. Cabernet Sauvignon and 2 ha. Syrah had been newly planted at the beginning of the 80s. The bodega was also equipped with modern installations and new oak vats were bought in France. New planting was done over an area of 15 ha., so that the total area of the vineyard amounted to more than 30 ha. In addition to this there were also 2,000 old olive trees on the domain and a few ha. of almond trees. These Arbequina olive trees now produce one of the best olive oils of the appellation Siurana, and is bottled under the name of 'Oli Mas d'en Gil'.
The domain is beautifully situated in a micro-climate in Bellmunt del Priorat, which is the lowest lying village with the highest temperatures of the DO Priorat. Because of their orientation towards the sea in the form of a basin, the vineyards benefit more from the 'Garbinada' or seabreeze, that provides coolness and humidity during the hot summer months. In this way the grapes undergo an optimum ripening. The terraces have been laid so as to preserve the basin shape, the micro-climate and the terroir in the most ideal way. This ensures that the tannins ripen well so that the wines are very pleasant to drink even when they are very young. Moreover, the terroir nuance guarantees them a long life. In addition to this, the low yields (17.5 hl for the oldest vines, and an average of 24.5 hl for the others), ensure an immense concentration of fruit. Here too the typical Priorat terroir, the llicorella or slate, produces the complex mineral touches in the wine.

Besides the llicorella vineyards there are also a number that have high levels of lime and iron. The first wines, which were produced on a very limited scale, were millésime 98, which was immediately a top quality millésime. The wines were the very first proof of the enormous potential of this domain and especially of the passion and knowledge that had been invested in its exploitation. Only 4,300 bottles were made of a white wine, the 'Coma Blanca', originating from 40 year old Garnache blanca (60%) and 45 year old Macabeo (40%). Always with a coupage that shows itself to the full; a white wine that is impressive and round. Macération pelliculaire was also used as well as a maturation of 6 months on new French oak.

The Mas d'en Gil domain is perfectly suited to the microclimate of the splendid Bellmunt del Priorat.

The red wines of Mas d'en Gil are also very impressive: the Coma Vella (15800 bottles) is a red wine with 40% Garnacha (30% Garnacha País, 10% Garnacha Peluda), 20% Carinena and the rest Cabernet Sauvignon and Syrah. The oldest vines were used for the Clos Fontà, with 60% Garnacha and 20% Carinena, to which 20% Cabernet Sauvignon was added from younger vines. These wines remain on French oak for 10 months (for the Clos Fontà 100% new). The two red wines are without doubt impressive. They are the best result of the 'second wave' of new Priorat. Of course this is not just a project, but the life's work of a man with a passion for wine and quality. After a lifetime of being active in wines from all over Spain, this domain is Rovira Rovira's dream, in which he can use his extensive experience in the service of these few top wines and take care of every detail no matter how minute. Here tradition and technology are used to their full potential.

Range

2 red wines

Mas d'en Gil, Coma Vella
30% Garnacha País, 10% Garnacha Peluda, 20% Cariñena,
25% Cabernet Sauvignon, 15% Syrah
10 months on French oak (new, second and third year)
Very dark in colour. Intense in the nose, blackberries, black currant, minerals, cocoa, and chocolate. Strong onset in the mouth with a lovely balance in the alcohol and the acids. Powerful finale.

Mas d'en Gil, Clos Fontà
40% Garnacha País, 20% Garnacha Peluda, 20% Cariñena, 20% Cabernet Sauvignon
Maturing of 10 months on new French oak
Ink-black. Intense nose of black fruit, black currant, liquorice and torrefaction, a great deal of terroir, lovely mineral tones. Heavy in the mouth, very expressively fruit, exuberant, powerful with a massive finale. Impressive.

1 white wine

Mas d'en Gil, Coma blanca
60% Garnacha blanca, 40% Macabeu
Intense straw-coloured yellow. Hints of spice in the nose, fennel, almonds, quince and honey. A strong onset in the mouth, plenty of alcohol and well supported with lots of material. Mineral tones. Very forceful ending, enormously long.

Export

The most important export countries are Belgium, Germany, Great Britain, USA and Switzerland.

Mas d'en Gil
VITICULTORS
Mas d'en Gil
PRIORAT
DENOMINACIÓ D'ORIGEN
PRIORAT
CLOS FONTÀ
EMBOTELLAT A
LA PROPIETAT
COLLITA
1998
7.300 Ampolles seleccionades
d'aquesta anyada
4628
43738 BELLMUNT DEL PRIORAT
PRODUCT OF SPAIN
R.S.I. 30-04267/CAT
R.E. 5627-T
75 cl.

Celler Bàrbara Forés

C. Santa Anna 28
CELLER BÀRBARA FORÉS
43780 Gandesa
Tel.: 977 42 01 60
Fax: 977 42 13 99

M. Carmen Ferrer and Manuel Sanmartín

Owners: Carmen Ferrer, Manuel Sanmartín

Oenologists: Carmen Ferrer, José-Luis Pérez

Agronomist: Carmen Ferrer

Surface: 18 ha. vineyard

Production: 19,000 bottles

Type: white, red, rosé

Entrance to the lovely town house. On the left are the cuves, and the vats on the right. Situated above are the living quarters.

The Terra Alta pioneers

Terra Alta is definitely one of Catalonia's nicest area's. It also feels a little left out: the comarca lies just over the river Ebro, more towards Valencia than towards Barcelona.

You follow the Ebro delta coastline towards the mainland, alongside the shimmering delta in Tortosa and its splendid nature parks. Hundreds of migrating birds overwinter here. Or they area on a stop-over on their way to Africa. Long veils of mist from the Ebro float over the countryside at dawn. At noon, the sun will be shining all over the fields and the neighbouring weathered rocks.

Gandesa is this peaceful comarca's capital, a small town of some 2,600 inhabitants. It is famous for its winemaking. The local cooperative houses in a quaint art-deco bodega with Gaudí roots. Most of this appellations 8,000 ha. vineyards' produce continues to be sold in bulk to the cava industry of Catalonia. The remainder is drunk by the local population. Very few bottles leave the area, in fact. If we look at the statistics we notice some 9,000 bottles were exported in 1998 (sic!) to countries abroad.

This is an area with huge possibilities, nevertheless. It borders onto the wild and rugged Aragon and its harsher climes to the West, to the North onto the slate-covered hills of warmer Priorat. The area is surrounded by the 'Beseit-mountains', the 'Serra de Pàndols' and the 'Serra de Cavalls'; it is crossed by 3 rivers, the Ebro and its two affluents, the Matarranya and the Algars. In terms of surface, the region is fairly limited; but it has many plantations and many ancient vines with lots of potential in them. It is the very picture of a Mediterranean landscape, has grain, olives and grapes. Its vineyards are sheltered from the North-West wind (the 'cerc, in Catalan language) by he sierra's. A cool South-West wind (the 'garbi' in Catalan) blows in the Ebro valley, bringing in the necessary freshness to fields. The vineyards are located some 300 to 600 m. high. What prevented Catalans producing famous wines so long, one wonders. Who or what could they have been waiting for?

Apparently, they were waiting for Carmen Ferrer! She was the first to prove the region is truly capable of producing top-class wines. And brilliantly so, at that!
The history of the Fores house indicates this to be no mere coincidence. The owners gave their wines the name of Carmen's great-grandmother: Bàrbara Forés (1828-1905) Her son, Rafael Ferrer, was a chemist and a wine-producer. He inherited the vineyards from her. Rafael was a visionary: he decided he wanted to do more with his vineyards than he saw being done around him. So, towards the end of the 19th century, he was the first to actually bottle his wine. He built a wine cellar in his house, adding fermentation casks and all that was necessary for the bottling process. A label dating back to those days can still be seen in the present-day bodega.
Carmen Ferrer and her husband, Manuel Sanmartín, too decided to take their in turn inheritance further. They live in Bàrbara Forés' and Rafael Ferrer's historic dwelling. A lovely townhouse with a nice entrance, to the center of Gandesa. The front door is to the back, via

Mainly new French oak is used for the maturing of the white and red wines. Here the vats are not stored in the cellar but in the house itself.

Everything is on a small scale here: the small cuves inox stand in what used to be the living area.

the little Calle Santa Anna. The hall refreshingly cool; all was carefully restored throughout the house. Carmen and Manuel's consider it their life's work. In one of the ground-floor rooms stand the inox casks: 2 tanks holding 10.000 l. each, 3 tanks of 5.000 l. each and 4 tanks with a capacity of 2.500 l. each. Everything is small-size: production is on the small scale here but begins with the Q of Quality. Barrels have been piled up in the next front-room: some 80 of them, practically all a 100% new, mainly French oak (Allier). The lovely, nicely tiled staircase leads to the lst and the 2nd floors that are residential quarters.
For Carmen and Manuel, the success story began in 1994, as they started to equip their house with the necessary wine-making tools. Never overlooking the old residence's existing structure. They did the restoration work themselves, little by little, using such means as were available. There is not the slightest pretention or arrogance about Carmen or Manuel. But they did make history for the step they took in 1994; for it turned out to be a kick-off for the entire appellation.
Carmen is a bio-engineer and a graduate oenologist. At first, she lectured at the Gandesa Institute. She then gave up her job to fully devote herself to the wine project she had in mind. Manuel had demanding activities: he was a lawyer and a communal secretary in the neighbouring village. But he too opted for the wine-making plan. In the beginning the couple even went from door to door selling their wine. People said they were mad: who was going to buy 800 Pesetas a wine you could find for 150 Pesetas at the coop?
But Carmen and Manuel's minds were focused on quality. They also had an eye for detail, simple notions no-one had been too familiar with in the area so far.
Their vineyards, mostly of a respectable age, are distributed all over Gandesa. Grapes come from a number of micro-climates, native soils, heights and sun-orientations. Their every facet finds expression in the wines.
A young white wine was the first to actually be bottled by them. It held 80% Garnacha blanca and 20% Macabeu. The grapes came from the 'Sénia de Tomaset', a vineyard close to the centre of Gandesa. It was a powerful white wine with lots of character. Carmen gave this wine a short 'macération pelliculaire' in order to add to its body. No more than 6,000 bottles were produced, rapidly followed by a rosé, a blend of Garnacha, Cabernet Sauvignon and Syrah, from mainly recent vines. Also a powerful wine with quite a structure of its own.
Carmen and Manuel knew the old Garnacha blanca vines had more in them. Terra Alta is used to being an area with Garnacja

blanca growing virtually wild. The grape is mostly resorted to for the making of 'rancio' wines or a sweet 'church-wine'. Carmen managed to have the old vines yield their best. In 1996, she created 'El Quintà', a strong white wine with storing qualities. (A 'Quintà' is a mostly small piece of land tended by the owner).This wine's grapes originated in 2 vineyards of 2 ha. each, close to Gandesa's 'Col d'Alsina'. The 'El Grau' vineyard has a fairly sandy soil with clay and a lot of chalk; the 'El Carrascal i la Cometa' has rocks and contains even more chalk. The vines are some 50 years old. They were thinned out by Carmen to manage producing quality from small cluster quantity. The 4 ha. give a mere 2 to 3,000 bottles. The grape itself is small and intensely sweet. The method used remaining the 'macération pelliculaire' followed by a first fermentation. The wine then is left to ferment on new French oak (Allier) and to ripen for another 6 months.

Appraisal and star-status only came when Carmen and Manuel put their red wine on the market. The wine was named after a vineyard, the 'Coma d'en Pou'. Its Cabernet Sauvignon vines (2 ha.) and Syrah's (1.5 ha.) yield particularly sweet fruit, blending well with the old Garnacha tinta variety of the 'Sénia de Tomaset' (1.5 ha.). The wine is given its malolactic fermentation on new French oak and ripens for some 12 months.

The result is one of the best red wines in Spain! Very Mediterranean in its style, also modern and 'international', seductive and lithe. Everyone likes it. Amateur buyers are queuing up but production is very restricted, unfortunately.

This is nevertheless the wine having connoisseurs admit the humble appellation held in more than anyone imagined! Carmen and Manuel's hard work and patience has not been in vain. For it has been an experience they wouldn't have missed for the world in the end. And Terra Alta now has its own firmly rooted 'superwine'!

Gandese, principal town of Terra Alta.

The discreet facade of Celler Bàrbara Forés: there is nothing to suggest the treasures that lie behind it.

Range

2 white wines

the white Bàrbara Forés
85% Garnacha blanca, 15% Macabeu
Bright yellow in colour. A fairly spicy nose at first turning florid later, with a number of dried fruit aroma's thrown in. A very strong start off in the mouth, lots of fruit, but very dry and powerful in structure. Long aftertaste with a firm annotation. Solely as an accompaniment for heavier meals. Character wine.

Bàrbara Forés, El Quintà
100% Garnacha blanca
A gown of yellow straw. Dazzling bouquet in the nose: ripe pears, quinces, almonds, cinnamon, coconut, exotic fruit. Very intricate. A nose leading to many a pleasurable hour. Strong palate not devoid of refinement. Loads of fruit, cleverly supported by delicate acids and nicely dosed wood. Mellow and plump with some grace in its body. The 'vieilles vignes de Grenache' are clearly present. Native tang wine. Long and lengthy aftertaste. A white wine ideally suited to white meat and fowl. Brilliantly authentic.

1 rosé

Bàrbara Forés rosat
34% Garnacha, 33% Cabernet Sauvignon, 33% Syrah
Pretty and lively dark pink gown. Ebullient nose of red fruit, mainly redcurrant. Fairly strong start-off by rosé standards. Nicely fruity in the mouth, sufficiently strong. Long and sophisticated aftertaste. An a-typical rosé wine.

1 red wine

Bàrbara Forés, Coma d'en Pou
50% Cabernet Sauvignon, 25% Garnacha, 25% Syrah
12 months on new French oak.
Deep dark red when poured out. An intricate and fine nose with masses of black and red fruit, delicate wood into the background, very pleasing and rich in minerals. An explosive fruit cocktail, balanced to the point of perfection: shiny fruits with ripe, assertive tannins and a sufficient amount of acids. Very intricate and elegant. A wine that has everything. Is tender and seductive. Long, over-indulging finale. Pure artistry. Exquisitely tasty, sinfully hedonic.

Export

50% of all production, mainly to Belgium, Denmark, Germany and Britain.

Celler
Bàrbara
Forés
1998
Coma d'En Pou
Bàrbara Forés
TERRA ALTA
DENOMINACIÓ D'ORIGEN
Gandesa - España
N.E-37.003.00 CAT

Costers del Siurana

Costers del Siurana
C. Manyetes
43737 Gratallops
Tel.: 977 83 92 76
Fax: 977 83 93 71
E-mail: costers@tinet.fut.es

The 'Costers del Siurana' team
Isidre, Iona, Mariona with little Joan,
Carles, Conso, Guillem and Joan.

Owners: Carles Pastrana, Mariona Jarque

Oenologists: Isidre Sanahujes, Joan Jarque, Mariona Jarque

Surface: 120 to 150 ha.

Production: 70,000 bottles

Type: 92% red
8% white

The steep Priorat terraces are a typical example of winegrowing in Costers del Siurana.

Local history re-written

The Spanish world of wine ought to raise a statue to Carles Pastrana and Mariona Jarque, the owners of Costers del Siurana. They gave the Priorat a new lease of life, with catalysis effect for remainder Spanish vineyard country. From 1991 onwards, it had Spain back onto the wine-world winners' podium.

Carles and Mariona were 27 and 19 respectively when the big adventure began. We note 1979. But it took them 10 more years to produce their first wine, the Clos de l'Obac 1989. It was not really a 'Priorat': its alcohol content attaining a mere 12.5%, – whilst a minimum of 13.5% is required by DO standards. The Clos de l'Obac 1989 might not have been a true Priorat, a couple of months after its first launching (in 1991) but the wine had been sufficiently approved by 'Slow Food' to be listed amongst the world's 150 best. Maybe we ought to keep in mind Costers del Siurana was officially founded on April 14th 1987...

What makes this particular Priorat region so special? First of all its history. A lot of wine was made here from old. A little river, the Siurana, crosses this up to 450 m. high country (hence the costers del Siurana name, 'sloping banks of the Siurana'), bordering onto the Sierra del Montsant (culminating point:1202 m.) to the North and the North-West, the Sierra de l'Argentera, Sierra Mola and Llavería (culminating point: 999 m.) to the East and the South-East; finally onto the valley of the Ebro, West and South.

Already by 1163 had Carthusian monks founded a monastery on the very spot where a shepherd had a vision of angles climbing stairs leading to heaven. The area's name is a reminder of this: the Scala Dei or the stairs leading to God'. The monastery was called Priorat de Scala Dei – a name the entire region was eventually known by. The monks laid on the vineyards; the area soon appeared to be wonderfully suited to the production of wine. It further survived the damage of time until about the midst of the 20th century. By then, the alcohol content of wine had dropped to a mere 17 to 18%; all the wines accused

Mas d'en Bruno, the domain of Miserere in Torroja del Priorat. The countryhouse that is being renovated dates from the 13th century and will house a small luxury hotel and restaurant.

rusticity and some were very badly processed. There no longer was any future in view for Priorat. The entire area was deserted.

Surviving on local harvests of almonds or grapes was hard in this low-yield cliff country. Many vineyards were remote; terraces at levels that were hard to reach were eventually abandoned, their vines (many ancient Garnacha's and Cariñena's) left to grow wild.

Priorat's main asset is its soil, unique in the world. It has a bottom-layer of almost exclusively slate (llicorella), rich in trace elements and minerals. This means vines can achieve perfect steadiness. Roots go foraging deep down. In quest of moisture and food, giving the wine its distinctive mineral content.

The Costers del Siurana project was to restore the wine tradition of Priorat to its former glory. When a group of idealists started to take it on (towards the end of the 70's and the early 80's), many shrugged their shoulders in disbelief; it would be a waste of time and money: had not Priorat country been in disrepute for a long time?... Slowly at first the old vineyards were re-acquired, brought back into shape, given additional species like Cabernet Sauvignon, Merlot and Syrah. The first 10 years remained difficult and thoroughly exhausting. But the powerful and strongly condensed wines finding their way to the cooperatives were tasty enough to have people realise there was hidden strength behind those vines, the

roots of which they practically felt growing under their feet! – More 'believers' joined in during the 80's. The group steadily grew: there were addicts from Britain, Belgium, Germany, France, but also Spain. Bundling their strength and know-how they prepared the take-off. Initially, the big adventure gathered some 10 members. By 1991 most members had gone their own way. In the end, only the Costers del Siurana itself had survived, with the Clos de l'Obac and Miserere, Clos Mogador, Clos Martinet and later the Finca Dofí.
With that success came a revival of interest, a strong echo of the former surrounding the Costers del Siurana project. This new movement took place in the mid-90's. Costers del Siurana also considered this is clear proof they had reached their target – and with light showing at the end of the tunnel!
Carles Pastrana and Mariona Jarque, the Costers del Siurana founders, are amongst the few to fully utilize grapes exclusively from own vineyards. The surface in ownership covers

Gratallops, centre of the new Priorat wines.

The winepress has been used for centuries to produce Priorat wines that are often strong and very alcoholic.

130 to 150 ha. Less than half is suited to the planting of vines. It moreover is a very demanding activity involving long hours with lots of hard work creating terraces, drilling holes in the cliffs and so on. A decent yield can only be expected after a number of years and it may stay on the narrow side for a very long time. Most new species, like Cabernet Sauvignon, Merlot and Syrah were added in the course of 1985 and 1986. They yield a mere 500 gr. to 1 kg. per plant. Grape quality is naturally higher this way, so is density. The Garnacha's and the Cariñena's nevertheless date back to 1900 and to the years in between 1945 and 1950. Hard work and trying circumstances are also a warrant as to high levels of satisfaction when results do occur!
Carles muses for a long time when he looks back on difficult days. But he also may well hold the keys to present-day Priorat success. It may well lay in those 10 lonely years preaching in the desert, the endless fending for survival, the ability to take it all in one's stride onto the path of misery and riches, anonymity and fame... The target has not changed: to produce an annual big keeper wine, with depth and native tang, has might have been done 9 centuries ago already, by the Carthusians of Priorat.
Clos de l'Obac and Miserere are more than worthy inheritors of the old traditional ways. The Clos de l'Obac grapes originate in different vineyards throughout Gratallops. The village turned into the 'Manhattan' of Priorat if landprices are anything to go by.

These particular wines' 'coupage' is the same for all: equal parts Garnacha and Cabernet Sauvignon and 3 smaller and equal parts Syrah, Cariñena and Merlot. A characteristic of their method being to plunge all the grapes in one same fermentation cask together. The

The 'Cemeterio' is the private cellar of Carles and Mariona where older vintages lie and mature.

coupage taking place in the very vineyard, no longer in barrels later. Maceration and fermentation happen at simultaneously; proceeding this way had salutary results. The wine then is layered on new French oak during 12 months.

A team of oenologists closely monitors the wine during the layering: firstly Isidre Sanahujes, responsible for vinifiation and undoutedly one of Spain's greatest oenologists. But also Mariona Jarque and her brother, Joan (both oenologists) make extensive contributions to the production process.

Clos de l'Obac may be their more famous wine: it certainly will not end there: another more recent project appears to clearly be in the lift: the 'Mas d'en Bruno', an estate of some 84 ha. in Torroja del Priorat, at 15 kms. from Gratallops. In 1976, Garnacha, Cabernet Sauvignon, Tempranillo, Merlot and Cariñena were planted there, as well as Garnacha blanca, Macabeo and Moscatel de Alejandría, if in lesser quantity. Another top-wine is produced here since 1990: the 'Miserere', a blend of above-mentioned grape species.

The estate with its gorgeous 13th century masía, lays at some 350 to 420 m. and is mainly South-East and South-West oriented. It produces wine considered to be less sturdy than the Clos de l'Obac on the whole, but is stronger on refinement. Up to now, wines were vinified in the Gratallops bodega. In time, the Miserere will have its own bodega in Mas d'en Bruno. Works already started to this effect and there are high hopes in the field of developments: besides a bodega there will also be a high-class restaurant and a small hotel with every possible luxury. The ground that was covered since 1979 – when there were very few means and possibilities but ambitions were so much the higher – is simply impressive.

Equally impressive is de Dolç de l'Obac, a sweet red wine basically Garnacha, Syrah and Cabernet Sauvignon. The limited amount of bottles it produces come from a 78 are vineyard. Grapes need late harvesting to better reach the desired 16 to 18% alcohol content. They then are layered on specially designed barrels of French oak where both maceration and fermentation take place. The wine further undergoes a 1% alcohol modification. Results, in one word, are heavenly: uncredibly rich in fruit content, nice sugars and acids, a hugely extensive aftertaste. The wine turned into a collector's item.
Another to soon make the grade may well be the Kyrie (a white wine this time), on the market in 2001. A mere foretaste reveals top-class. Quantities will be very limited considering no more than some 5% of all vineyard surface has white grapes.

A joint characteristic of the wines Isidre Sanahujes produces is their elegance and refinement. Piece by piece they are the rough boys fitted into silk gloves. There is a style that cannot be equaled in Priorat, -though many may have tried!

Carles and Mariona wrote wine-history for an area the importance of which turned out crucial for Spain. Only after the first Priorat successes did the new Rioja and Ribera del Duero projects truly take off too. They gave a dying area new lease of life, – something both Catalonia and Spain may be grateful for.

In spite of all compliments and praise, Carles and Mariona are with both feet firmly on the ground, discrete, without the slightest pretention and open-minded as ever. But now looking ahead to the future with the same amount of ideal and new plans as before. And the Costers del Siurana project is young. In other words: there is a bright future ahead!

Range

Red wines

Usatges negre
Garnacha, Cabernet Sauvignon, Merlot, Cariñena, Tempranillo, Syrah
12 months French oak, new, second and third year
Bright red in colour. Strong blackcurrant nose, black fruit and fine mineral touches. Sensitive and elegant palate with enough filling and fruit. Well structured acids. Needs time. Nice aftertaste.

Miserere
Garnacha, Cabernet Sauvignon, Tempranillo, Cariñena, Merlot
12 months French oak, new and second year
Bright red in colour. Black y nose with lots of minerals, blackcurrant, liquorice and delicate wood. A fine start-off in the mouth, plenty of red tannins and masses of black fruit, goes very far. Very equilibrated. Grand finale. Native tang.

Clos de l'Obac
Garnacha, Cabernet Sauvignon, Syrah, Cariñena, Merlot
12 months new French oak
Deep red in colour. Intricate black fruit nose, blackcurrant, flint, cocoa, leather and minerals. A strong start-off in the mouth but not without sophistication, acid tannins and fruit in perfect proportion. Huge length. A wine for hedonic intellectuals.

White wine

Usatges blanc
Garnacha blanca, Macabeu, Moscatel de Alejandría
8 months on new French oak
Bright yellow when poured out. A nose needing time: fairly tight at first, with minerals, citrus, frangipane, coconut and apple. A perfect symbiosis of strength and elegance in the mouth. Big finale. A grand white wine.

1 sweet wine

Dolç de l'Obac
Garnacha, Syrah, Cabernet Sauvignon
12 months new French oak, maceration and fermentation on oak
A gown of black ink. Terrific nose of sweet bramberry, bilberry, tomato, basil, cocoa, chocolate, blackcurrant, coffee and cinnamon. Heaps of fruit in the mouth, 16,5% of thoroughly integrated alcohol, nicely charming, the peak of elegance and refinement. Endless aftertaste. A pure sang for the pleasure of it.

Export

60% goes abroad, mainly the USA, Britain, Germany, Japan, Switzerland and the Benelux.

Costers
CLOS DE L'OBAC
EMBOTELLAT A LA PROPIETAT
PRIORAT
Costers del Siurana
Propietari Pastrana & Jarque
75 cl
PRODUCT OF SPAIN
13,5% vol
ELABORAT, CRIAT I EMBOTELLAT PELS CELLERS
Costers del Siurana
43737 Gratallops - Spain
R.E. 6737-T
L-1

Abel Mendoza

Ctra. Peñacerrada 7
Abel Mendoza
26338 San Vicente de la Sonsierra
Tel.: 941 30 80 10
Fax: 941 30 80 10
E-mail: jarrarte@detelogic.es

Abel Mendoza

Owner: Abel Mendoza Monge

Oenologist: Maite Fernández

Agronomist: Abel Mendoza

Surface: 16 ha. in ownership

Production: 70,000 bottles

Type: 98% red
2% white

1988. This is the year in which the small bodega was founded.

A father to his vines

Abel Mendoza does not readily seek the limelight. Even in Rioja, where everyone knows everyone else, he remains relatively unknown. Only the bodegueros, who are every bit as perfectionist when it comes to their vineyards, nod in acknowledgment when you mention 'Abel Mendoza'.
It may be a characteristic of those taking their work seriously: they know and appreciate each other! This is also the case for Rioja. In spite of the fact that, in the area, most estates appear to be producer 'crazy', to the point their only concern appears to be the quantity. Particularly at a time when some of the estates are trying to return the necessary fame to the appellation adding quality, this is a truly sad state of affairs.
Abel too is disconsolate as we drive past the vineyards; vines are heavy with grapes: all bumper size and to be sold at a good price to the large estates later. Quality does not really come into it: producing the necessary documents certifying DOC-qualification will do the trick with the big houses of Rioja.

Abel Mendoza's point of view is a totally different one: he owns a mere 16 ha. in vineyard land, scattered throughout the commune of San Vincente de la Sonsierra, towards the outer border of 2 subsidiary area's, Rioja Alta and Rioja Alavesa. More than anything in the world, Mendoza cares for his vines. 26 small vineyards, sometimes less than 1 ha. in size, harbour a true treasure in the way of old stock. The soil contains vast amounts of chalk, clay and stones. The age of the vines varies from 70 (the oldest) to 2 (latest additions).

Abel has clear-cut theories as far as the caring for his vines is concerned. Not one, even the smallest bunch of grapes is covered up. In vineyards of his, every cluster reaches out freely into the open, leaving the fruit well aired. Excess leaves and fruit are removed, the remainder is clearly visible. The air must manage circulating well to prevent the fruit rotting. 70,000 bottles have been the result of his method so far, the greater part of which is put on the local market in the way of a young, fruity 'macération carbonique' wine. The best is put on the

The river Ebro that flows through La Rioja and plays an essential role in local winegrowing.

Dotted among the vineyards are the old stone huts that were used as shelters for the harvesters in bygone days.

market as 'Jarrarte Crianza'; there are no more than 8,000 bottles of it. It furthermore remains the only exported vintage. A new wine was put on the market just recently: the Abel Mendoza Selección Personal, a small part of which originated in the 'El Bardallo' vineyard with Tempranillo 40 to 50 years old (and potentially the best), reserved the making of this wine. The first millésime was 1998. A Rioja pearl.

Abel is also unique in producing an outstanding white wine out of old Malvasia. The Malvasía used to be widespread in Rioja in the past. But it systematically disappeared out of the vineyards. Here and there, a few, fortunately, did survive. Abel considers the Malvasia vineyard his 'capricho personal', -one that yields a mere 1,000 bottles. The wine goes through a fermentation process in casks of new French oak and keeps its fermentation cells over a number of months whilst in barrel. A couple of months in the bottle and out comes the proof Abel Mendoza's theory Rioja also manages some delightful white wines was absolutely right!

Abel writes his wine labels by hand. You might think so much dedication would be crowned by the Rioja Consejo Regulador; you may also be wrong: because such labels do not conform to norms on the subject, this excellent white wine could not go on the market. Most bottles had already left for export when the interdiction came through, however – in the circumstances, this is just as well…!

Abel had similar problems with his red wine, the Selección Personal: he wanted to mention the name of the grape producing vineyard, 'finca el Bardallo' on the label. This wasn't on, said the Consejo Regulador. Spain may well follow Italy, in that sense: anyone who really wants to make good wine without taking too many rules into account to start off with might just as well sell it as vino de mesa or as table wine at once…

Best of all: owing to widespread mass production many houses annually bring out millions of bottles of a very

Old Tempranillo vines with San Vicente de la Sonsierra in the background.

dubious quality; but all is done according to the rules of the Consejo Regulador. The appellation myth in the field of certificate of quality losing quite a few of its feathers in the process...

Already as a child, Abel Mendoza liked to do little jobs in the his father's vineyards, tending the vines. On inheriting, he continued to bestow the same care on them he had watched his father do.
In 1988 – he was 19 – he decided to bottle wine himself and put an own brand on the market, a wine called 'Jarrarte' (after one off his smaller vineyards). Only young and fruity 'macération carbonique' wines were made until 1994. That very year (one of Rioja's best), he decided to add a crianza wine to his collection, – but it was not to be like everybody else's! Traditional Rioja crianza wines are mainly light, practically devoid of body and structure. They are stored in old casks of American oak. The result is a musty, oxidized cocktail, annually drunk by millions of Spaniards (some people even pretend to find it nice).
But Abel invested his money in buying barrels of new French oak: he hated to see his grapes, lovingly tended all the year through, spoilt through the stale wood of old American barrels. His relatives said he was mad: they feared the wine would be much to expensive this way. No-one would buy it anymore, they said – and Abel would ruin himself and his family in the process. We know by now nothing of the sort happened. Thanks to his never failing concern and his unshakable faith in quality, Abel Mendoza currently belongs to the narrow elite of the top quality producers in Rioja.

Range

3 red wines

Jarrarte, tinto joven
95% Tempranillo, Graciano, Garnacha
Bright red in colour. 'Macération carbonique' nose with lots of sweet things and red forest fruit. Pleasant to the palate with much fruitiness and fraîcheur. Sophisticated aftertaste.

Jarrarte, crianza
98% Tempranillo, Graciano, Garnacha
12 months French oak, including ⅓ new and the remainder in the 2nd and the 3rd year
Dark red in colour. Fairly tight nose opening up when aired. Intensely fruity, redcurrants, bramberries, raspberries, blackcurrants and candied fruits of the forest, a touch of leather and cocoa. Many minerals, a great deal of native tang. Similar palate leading to a rich start off and plenty of fruit in midriff. Cleverly dosed acids. Lengthy finale. A true native.

Abel Mendoza, Selección Personal
100% Tempranillo
12 months new French oak
Dark in colour. Young nose, intense and intricate, mainly fruit and mineral overtones with a pleasant and (discreet) discrete touch of wood into the background. Cocoa, leather. Spiciness. Very delicate and elegant palate, subdued robustness perfectly cast and structured, ripe tannins and intensely precise acids. Sophisticated and drawn out aftertaste. A paragon of finesse and native tang!

1 white wine

Abel Mendoza, Malvasía fermentado en barrica
100% Malvasía
4 to 6 months in new French oak 'sur lies'
Bright yellow in colour. Discrete nose, spicy, citrus overtones, fine exotic fruit, orange peel, a very delicate touch of wood, minerals. Herby flavour to start off with, lots of fruit in its midriff, perfect wood-fruit balance, nice acids.
Many native tang touches. Long and sophisticated aftertaste. A wine that is quite unique, wonderfully well balanced.

Export

20% for export, mainly the Crianza wines: Germany, the USA, Belgium, France, Denmark.

RIOJA
Abel Mendoza
RIOJA
Denominación de Origen Calificada

Fernando Remírez de Ganuza

Constitución 1
Fernando Remírez de Ganuza
01307 Samaniego
Tel.: 941 60 90 22
Fax: 941 12 33 35
E-mail: redeganuza@eniac.es

Fernando Remírez de Ganuza

Owner: Fernando Remírez de Ganuza

Oenologist: Pablo Martínez

Agronomist: Fernando Remírez de Ganuza

Area: 53 ha.

Production: between 30.000 and 110.000 bottles

Type: red, mainly Reserva

The selection table where the 'shoulders' are cut from the 'points'.

Revolutionary in selection and quality

Fernando Remírez de Ganuza is a man with vision. Without ever having been educated as a master of agricultural science, there are few in Rioja who have as much experience as he in vineyards. Remírez de Ganuza founded his own domain in 1989. Before this he had always been active in the world of wine, especially in the 'vineyard business'. Born in Meano in Navarra, he was involved at an early age in Rioja, in the buying and selling of vineyards. The experience he acquired here proved to be extremely useful when giving form to his idea. The idea was as simple as it was brilliant: only the best is good enough. And you only get the best if you are very strict in your selection.

This selection is Fernando's hobby. Proudly he shows us the double selection table. All the bunches of grapes find their way here and after a meticulous double check, are cut into two. Only the top section of the bunch ('los hombros', literally meaning 'the shoulders') are used to make his famous Reserva, which is the flagship of the bodega. The lower section of the bunch ('los puntos') are either sold or used by Fernando to make the R (erre punto), a wine made using the macération carbonique method which is traditional in Rioja. The lower parts of the bunch are indeed more suitable for making a macération carbonique (hence the name).

Fernando did the rest: 100 kg grapes from the upper section of the bunch produce 6 kg of green stalks; 100 kg grapes from the lower section of the bunch produce barely 1 kg of green stalks... A macération carbonique that is made with only the lower sections therefore produces more fruit and fewer vegetal tones. However the wine is not exported. The price abroad would be too high for a young 'vin de macération carbonique'. Fernando is a ready consumer of this wine, and when served cool and in the typical 'porron', the summer passes far more pleasantly for him.

The fact that Fernando Remírez de Ganuza cuts the bunch of grapes in two is not simply a gratuitous fad, but the result of years of experience with grapes and vinifications in other vineyards and other bodegas. Through systematically tasting grapes, he discovered that there was a considerable difference in ripeness and flavour between the grapes at

Fernando Remírez de Ganuza on his domain
in the charming village of Samaniego

the top of the bunch and those at the bottom. Moreover, the lower grapes are far dirtier since rainwater drains off via the lower part of the bunch. Consequently there are great advantages to using the top grapes only.

All the different stages of the vinification are the result of Fernando's years of experience and his logical thought processes. But in his view little has changed in vinification over the years: the main difference being that now things are done properly. This has involved a change in mentality with regard to both wine making and the consumer. Nevertheless there are still very few domains in Rioja where things are done really 'well'.

Infected by the success of pioneers like Fernando Remírez de Ganuza en Roda, more and more traditional domains are also making a 'super cuvée', and setting up a selection table mainly for the purpose of looking good in photographs in commercial brochures, after which these 'super cuvées' are sold at prices that bear no relation to their quality. This is an unfortunate development which of course will be short-lived: quality always shows itself in the glass and the truth of this will reveal itself more and more clearly over the years. This down-to-earth analysis of the present 'super cuvée boom' is shared by Pablo Alvarez of Vega Sicilia in Ribera del Duero.

This apparently explains why the best known American wine guru described Remírez as the Latour of Spain. That is quite a compliment. The Reservas of Remírez de Ganuza are so perfectly structured that they will easily withstand the test of time. On the other hand, Fernando is also against the trend of uniformity that came into being through the influence of Parker. An excess in concentration and wood do nothing to benefit the long life of the wine. And yet this is increasingly the style being adopted by young wine makers.

However, Fernando's inventiveness does not end with the selection. The fermentation vats are also different to those used on most domains. There are different types on the domain, all of which are fairly small. There are the traditional wooden vats made from French oak, which are similar to those used in Roda and Artadi, as well as cuves inox which he has specially made in the form of a cone that becomes narrower towards the top, so that the contact with the skins at the bottom is more intense. In addition to this he also has his own special method for pressing the grapes: He lowers a bag into the vat that is gradually filled with water. In this way the pressure is evenly distributed. In this way the pressing is continuous and there is no interposing of oxygen, thereby rendering a greater extraction possible.

The wine then matures in oak vats, of which 70% is French and 30% American. Most of the vats are new, but there are a number of old vats so as to maintain an equilibrium with regard to the influence of the wood. The wine remains on the wood for 25 to 28 months, which

might appear to be a very long period. However the latest vintages show an exceptional fruit expression and that the wood is extremely well integrated.
However this method of working and the exclusive selection do have a price with regard to the production. Let us do a re-run: only 17,000 bottles were made from the first vintage 1993. Neither '91 nor '93 were commercialised. During the top years of '94 and '95, 87,000 and 70,000 bottles respectively were produced. 1996 was a very good year but the selection should have been more rigid: 62,000 bottles. '97 was a very difficult year for many in Rioja. However, Fernando's '97 is sublime: after selection he made less than 30,000 bottles. Whereas other bodegas increase their production each year, here the number of bottles decreases annually! Fortunately things changed in the top year of '98. About 110,000 bottles of '98 will be put onto the market.
By now Fernando owns about 53 ha., almost all with vines more than 30 years old. 90% of the grapes are Tempranillo, and the rest mainly Graciano. These 53 ha. are the nec plus

Fernando's best vineyard at La Iglesia del Sotillo

The name of the bodega, beautifully engraved by an ornamental metalworker.

ultra of the Rioja Alavesa region. Because Fernando worked for many years buying and selling vineyards, many hundreds of ha. have passed through his 'hands'. He was therefore in a better position to keep the better vineyards for himself. One of the very best vineyards is situated just below 'La Iglesia del Sotillo', only 100 metres distant from the bodega in the heart of Samaniego. A special pruning technique is used in this vineyard instead of the traditional method of pruning first into two and then three points. The vineyard lies in a picturesque valley with a view of the historical buildings of the bodega.
From the moment that Fernando decided to make wine himself, it was clear that he would go and live in the bodega. The Family Remírez moved from Logroño to the small town of Samaniego. Fernando lives and works in the bodega and is very involved in his wines. It is therefore not surprising that his warm personality and openness is also expressed in his wines. The manner of working here is clearly different from the rest. Not only the wines are great, but the personality of their maker is also expressed in a top quality that is very evident.

Range

2 red wines

R. ('Erre Punto')
Tempranillo (almost 100%)
The macération carbonique wine for local use, made from the 'puntos' of the bunch of grapes (hence the name). Beautiful dark red colour. In the nose an explosion of forest fruits, strawberries, raspberries. No trace of any immaturity. The fruit stays in the mouth with a strength that we do not expect a wine like this to have. Elegant and fruity aftertaste.

Remírez de Ganuza Reserva
90 à 95% Tempranillo, otherwise Graciano, Garnacha, Mazuelo.
Deep red warm colour. A lovely spiciness in the nose, with plenty of black fruit. Complex touches of minerals (terroir), black liquorice, leather, but at the end it is mainly the black fruit that keeps coming back. Forceful onset in the mouth, with an enormous concentration of fruit. Elegants acids and juicy tannins. Enormous length. Long shelf life. A great wine.

Export

50% of the production: 25% USA, 25% Europe

Remírez de Ganuza
RIOJA
Denominación de Origen Calificada
• Reserva 1995 •
Este vino ha sido elaborado
y embotellado en la propiedad.
Bodegas Fernando Remírez de Ganuza, S.A.
Samaniego - Rioja Alavesa - España
75cl.
14 % vol.

Artadi

Ctra. Logroño
ARTADI
01300 Laguardia
Tel: 941 60 01 19
Fax: 941 60 08 50

Juan Carlos López de Lacalle

Owners: 3 cosechero's, headed by Juan Carlos López de Lacalle

Daily guide: Jean-François Gadeau

Oenologists: Benjamin Romeo, Jean-François Gadeau, Juan Carlos López

Surface: 180 supervised ha., including 50 ha. in ownership

Production: 500,000 bottles (the 'cosecheros Alaveses' are further bottled by the million under a variety of brandnames)

Type:	99%	red, including a small quantity top wines
	0,6%	white
	0,3%	rosé
	0,1%	Cava (méthode champenoise)

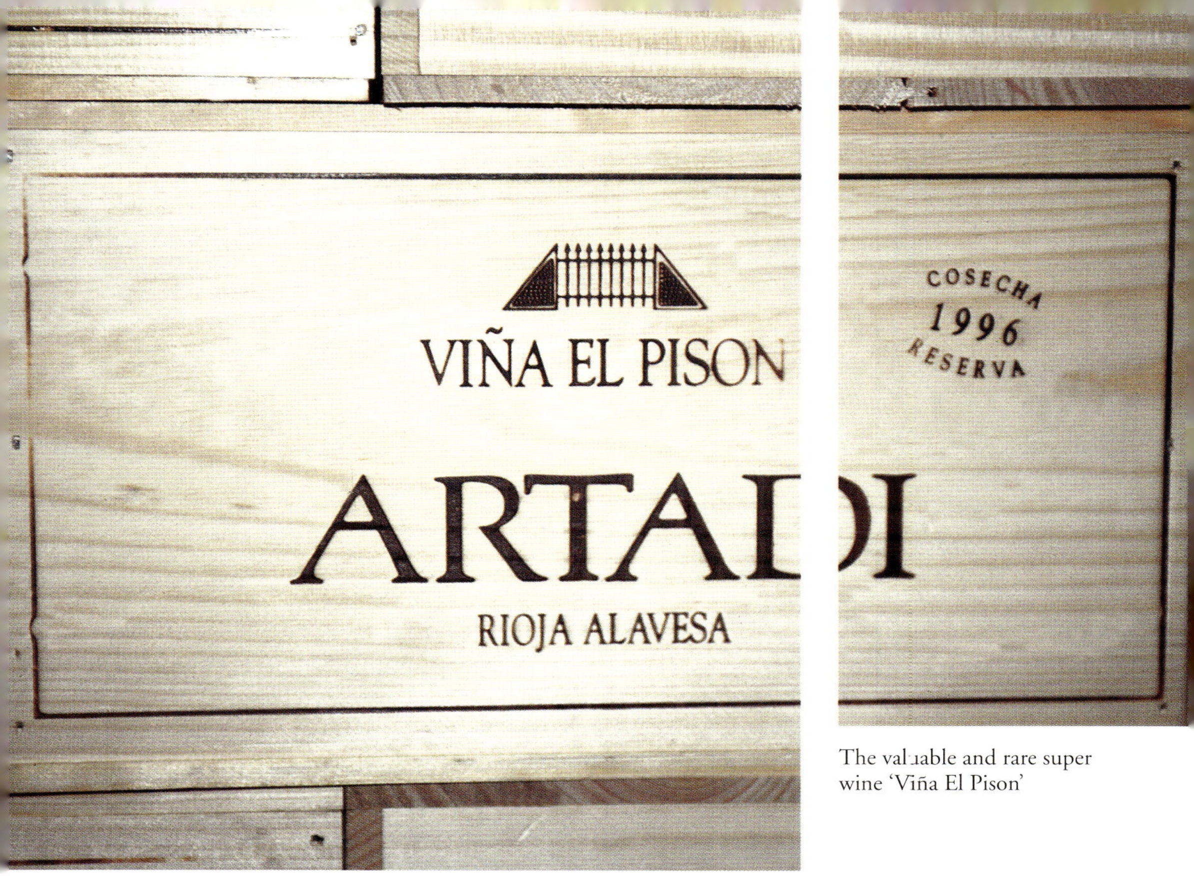

The valuable and rare super wine 'Viña El Pison'

From 'vino de cosechero' to 'vino de autor'

You might say the little Laguardia village is the 'capital' of the Rioja Alavesa area. This is the part of Rioja stretching to the Basque province Alava, North-East of the appellation. The area traditionally produces 'cosecho'wines. These are young and fruity wines obtained the macération carbonique way. Many small scale wine-producers or 'cosecheros' used to manage this themselves, with the help of primitive technical equipment; or they sold their grapes to the cooperative.
At the start of the '80's, a number of cosecheros began clubbing together to find a way to jointly bottle their wines. A cooperative was set up in 1985, gathering 15 members under the name 'Cosecheros Alavesas'. From the beginning they produced a young cosechero wine using the traditional 'macération carbonique' method. This young Tempranillo wine was put on the market under the name Artadi and soon turned into a reference of quality. It was mainly under Juan-Carlos López de Lacalle's impulse the idea of 'taking things further' began to take shape. Was not Juan Carlos, indeed, one of the very first to discover the entire area's possibilities? The riches of the old Tempranillo wine vines held in far more than young annual Artadi wine!

So, in 1990, the Pagos Viejos was vinified for a first time. After some 3 years it headed for the market under the Reserva label. Another first class wine followed in 1992, from grapes originating in one same vineyard: Viña El Pisón. Then, in 1994, the house presented its masterpiece: the Grandes Añadas. These 3 wines turned into the bodega's strengths. Summa cum laude raining down on them, led by the 99 marks the US wine-guru, Robert Parker, gave the El Pisón 1995 – the highest ever scored by a Spanish wine.

The Viña El Pisón comes from a single 2.8 ha. vineyard harbouring mainly Tempranillo wine vines, planted in 1945. The soil is a mixture of clay and chalk with high calcium carbonate content. The annual yield reaches the 3,000 to 3,500 kgs per ha. land. The vineyard is the property of Juan Carlos himself and the wine will no longer appear under the Artadi

One of the old Tempranillo vines in the 'El Pison' vineyard

Viña El Pison, walled in like a 'clos' and closed off by the gate that is also depicted on the label.

label in future, but under the name Viñedos Lacalle y Laorden S.A.. One of the vineyard's characteristics appears to be a wall surrounding it everywhere, like a true 'clos'. The Viña El Pisón label shows a gate closing the vineyard. In fact, some little old gate is being pictured here that was made out of the iron rods of a barrel dismantled by one of Juan Carlos' ancestors. The 'clos' limited surface also means the annual production of the El Pisón is

The treasures of Artadi lie maturing in the cellar.

restricted indeed, no more than 8 or 9,000 bottles annually leaving the estate.The larger part immediately going to the USA, Britain and Switzerland. The wine is a rarity, even in Spain.

Another rarity is the Grandes Añadas, on the market for the 2nd time in the year 2000. The wine ought to be the estate's summit (El Gran Vino de Artadi) and is solely produced during the best harvest years (until now: 1994 and 1998). The grapes are selected from vines over the 50 years old; the Pagos Viejos is usually made from these.

1994 was a spectacular year: the wine had so much body there was a need to use 200% new French oak. New oak for the first year and new oak again in the following culture year. That wine too turning into a Reserva in the classic sense, this way – the law on Rioja Reserva wines stipulates they may only be put on the market in their 3d year, after a barrel-ripening of 12 months minimum, using oak casks. In practice most Reserva's from Rioja stay a mere 24 months on oak, something not necessarely improving the quality of most traditional Rioja wines.

The typical Rioja notions like Reserva, Crianza and Gran Reserva are nevertheless resolutely overthrown from millésime 1998 onwards. Artadi definitely opting for renewal, whereby the name Reserva gets firmly discarded in the cases of the Pagos Viejos, the Viña El Pisón and the Grandes Añadas. Like Finca Allende and Abel Mendoza, Artadi ranks amongst those few wine houses deviating from the rules imposed by the Consejo Regulador de la Rioja in the field of culture. According to Juan Carlos, the law on denominations is an outdated notion. The wine itself will determine as to how long it is to remain on wood. Neither does Juan Carlos hide the fact he is very Bordeaux-minded. This French approach is also found in the house's commercial exchanges: Artadi is Rioja's first bodega to sell its top wines as 'primeurs' to its regular clientèle. An explanation of the French influence may well be the fact a Frenchman took over the daily running of the estate: Jean-François Gadeau is more than the oenologist (a function he shares with Benjamin Romeo): he was recently appointed the bodega's manager.

Jean-François is a pragmatic Frenchman with his own view of the new generation Spanish wines. He maintains there has never really been evolution in traditional Spanish wines. Whilst, in other countries (mostly France, in this case), the very notion of tradition went together with permanent growth. Under Franco's

dictatorship any form of renewal was systematically blocked – this was also the case for the wine sector, making evolution in tradition difficult. Remodelling the world of wine staying entirely dependent on changes in the political sphere. Only by chance did things start to move again in 1986-'87 with Spain's entry into the European Community.

Jean-François estimated results – attained by Rioja today! – could not be so far off: there must be true identification of possibilities and firmly, factually translating these, with a practical and modern approach. 'Modern' did not necessarely mean the more 'traditional' elements of vinification were to be left out: the house's 3 major wines do not undergo fermentation in inox casks but in large French oak fermentation tanks. These are intelligently used in a way to have the wine itself determine its own potential. All wines then get layered on new French oak (in the case of top wines) and on French oak from the 2nd, 3rd and 4th year (cfr. the Viñas de Gain).

The Sierra Cantabria, bordering on the Rioja region with an exquisite view of the Rioja Alavese. Mist covers the Basque Country but cannot cross over the Sierra Cantabria.

Artadi's final target is doublefold: to bring out the Tempranillo wine's aroma to the full and having a wine that, whilst thoroughly structured, remains delicately sophisticated and maintains a certain amount of freshness. The Atardi wines confirming a number of times efforts on their behalf were in no way in vain: quality stays the best guarantee for the future, also in Rioja Alavesa!

Range

Cava

Cava, Artadi Reserva Brut
100% Viura
Once in a while are produced a few hundred bottles Cava. This is a pleasant, neatly sparkling wine, the taste of which has every distinctive Viura characteristic.

White wines

Artadi blanco cosecha
100% Viura
A white wine, young and cool, with a lovely clear transparency. Pleasantly spicy, it leaves a flowery aftertaste in the mouth.

Artadi, Viñas de Gain blanco fermentado en barrica
100% Viura
(Has a yellow shiny straw robe.) Yellow-straw coloured gown. Pleasant vanilla touches in the mouth with masses of white fruit, apple and quince, nicely spiced into the background. Fairly mellow and firm palate. Lovely aftertaste of sharp acids and a dash of bitterness.

Rosé wijn

Artadi Rosado Cosecha
98% Tempranillo, 2% Viura
Bright pink in colour. Nose of summery fruits and flowers. A pleasant freshness in the mouth.

Red wines

Artadi, Tinto Cosecha
98% Tempranillo, 2% Viura
Purple-red in colour, typical macération carbonique nose. Fruity palate with a cool finale.

Artadi, Viñas de Gain Crianza
98% Tempranillo, 2% Graciano, Garnacha, Mazuelo
Bright red in colour. Finely streamlined nose of red fruit with hints of cocoa and chocolate. Perfectly balanced acids and equilibrium in fruitiness with lots of French oak. Full-bodied palate with a nicely equilibrated finale.

Artadi, Pagos Viejos
98% Tempranillo, 2% Graciano, Garnacha, Mazuelo
Deep red in colour. Fine black fruit nose and a background of minerals, opening up on shaking and swirling. Powerful palate but not without class or finesse. Structured to the very point of perfection. Sophisticated and lengthy finale.

Artadi, Grandes Añadas
100% Tempranillo
(Robe of deep red-ink.) Deep red inky gown. A wine like a bombshell, heavily concentrated. Very rich in black fruit, a nose of chocolate and vanilla. Nice start off. Full-bodied and powerful in the mouth, thoroughly structured and rich. A sophisticated finish hugely drawn out. Grandee.

Viñedos De Lacalle y Laorden, Viña El Pisón
99% Tempranillo, 1% Graciano
Dark red in colour. Very fine nose of great intricacy. A pinnacle of structure and refinement to the palate, mineral touches and black fruit, with an infrastructure of nicely dosed, new French oak. Full and concentrated. Long, pleasant finale. Grand, powerful, thoroughly sophisticated structure.

Export

50% of all export goes to the USA, Britain and Switzerland.

ARTADI
A
Grandes Añadas
Reserva 1994
Rioja
ARTADI

Roda

Avenida Vizcaya 5, Barrio de la Estación,
RODA
26200 Haro
Tel.: 941 30 30 01
Fax: 941 31 27 03
E-mail: rodarioja@roda.es

Isidro Palacios, Carlos Diez and Agustín Santolaya, Rioja's 'dreamteam'

Owners: Mr. and Mrs. Rotllant-Daurella

Daily guide: Agustín Santolaya

Oenologists: Agustín Santolaya, Carlos Diez

Oenologist and agronomist: Isidro Palacios

Oenologist and chemical analyst: Esperanza Tomás

Surface: 72,42 ha. in ownership

Production: 140,000 bottles (projection for 2004: 280,000 bottles)

Type: red, mainly Reserva

The cellars of Roda have been hewn into the rock in the Barrio de la Estación of Haro.

Pioneers in perfection

Roda is undeniably the pioneer of the Rioja region's revival. Thanks to the success of Roda, many estates followed the leader onto the 'new' Rioja wine path. At a time when every true connoisseur had already given up Rioja as a quality appellation was launched the first Roda I, Reserva 1992. The wine sparked off a comeback as never before into the Rioja wine region.

It all began in the mid-80's, when Mr. and Mrs. Rotllant-Daurella, from Catalonia, unfolded a wine-project to truly add to the Spanish vinicultural landscape of the day. Mario Rotllant is a successful Catalan businessman, active in a number of enterprises and sectors, including the distribution of leading French wines in Spain (besides Spanish top-class wines such as the famous Clos de l'Obac from Priorat). The RODA project – the appellation contains the joint names of the owners – was to see the day in the 'Barrio de la Estación' of the small town Haro (Rioja Alta area), more or less the centre of traditional Rioja. With some well established choice-classics as its closest neighbours: Muga, López de Heredia and La Rioja Alta.

Roda was set up in 1987. Its aim was perfection every inch of the way whilst processing, from beginning to end. Very little was to be overlooked. A team of 4 oenologists was set up, leaving nothing to chance: Agustín Santolaya and Carlos Diez, two technical engineers, Isidro Palacios, an agricultural engineer and Esperanza Tomás, a chemical engineer. After some experiments in vinification, the team was to produce a first Roda, tough not actually materializing until 1992. Involved was a starter-batch of only 60,000 bottles. At the time, even this small amount had unprecedented repercussions on the Spanish market. It was also the result of the philosophy backing this wine, an affair that was unique for Rioja, still considered the cradle of Spanish wine. For Roda started with the grape. This might seem quite obvious…Not so in Rioja: the area had been a typical 'négociant' appellation from old. Its wine-growers exploited their few ha. land to sell as much of their grape production as possible to the bodega's. Facing them were the bodega's oenologists. They

Old Tempranillo vines on the border of the Rioja region

considered the wine making process only began being interesting once the tractor with grapes actually reached the bodega.
Up to this day (95% of all bodega's still functions this way), wine-growers and oenologists continue to lead a parallel existence in Rioja. But Roda held a warrant for the entire philosophy: perfection, from the grape-stage itself to the moment trained cellarers presented the bottle in the most famous restaurants everywhere. And the world of wine was turned upside down, Roda being prepared to pay the wine-growers far more for quality than for quantity!
With a hint of melancholy in his smile, Agustín Santolaya, manager of the estate, shows us the posters on grape purchase that were put up in every village at the start of the operation. Not only would much more be paid for quality grapes from vines over 30 years old, but the

payment would be cash. Whilst, up to now, wine-growers could only expect their money after so many months, as a rule…
Today, Roda owns over 72 ha. land, furthermore surveying another 100 ha., and applying a system of long term contracts. Each wine-grower proceeds according to Roda guidelines. Production, in the meanwhile, attained the 140,000 bottle figure, – a minimum by Rioja standards. Mostly involved is Tempranillo wine from the Rioja Alta vineyards. Only the Garnacha comes from Tudelilla, in Rioja Baja. For grapes ripen better in there. Agustín Santolaya also strongly believes in the Graciano, a variety with such a longstanding history in Rioja it never really died out. The latest Graciano vines are nevertheless still too young for decent results. One of the bodega's basic principles remaining not to resort to grapes from vines less than 30 years old. The average age of the vines even climbing up to the 55 figure.

A vin de château had basically been aimed at, made out of grapes from vineyards surrounding the Haro bodega. But such vineyards spread over several soils for practical reasons. For Roda borders onto the Sierra Cantabria that, geographically speaking, is considered a natural border for the culture of grapes. In summer most of all, clouds can be seen gathering towards the edge of the Sierra Cantabria. The mist descends from the heights onto the vineyards at dawn, bringing in the necessary moisture. Clouds and rain stay behind the mountain tops. More often than not the sun breaks through mid-morning, dispersing the last

Standing between the vineyards are the age-old stone huts used by shepherds and harvesters.

Every vineyard has its own vegetation cycle. The ground vegetation is preserved up to a certain point so that the roots have to delve even deeper for their nutrition. Moreover, certain plants in the ground covering supplement the nutrition of the vines with certain elements and minerals.

shreds of mist. Since one same place and soil might represent far too big a risk in the field of annual top quality warranty, research was conducted to identify 12 different places, each containing another kind of 'top soil'. This research was inspired by the classification methods applied in the Douro region of Portugal. Various parameters were involved, each one important in its own right: the geology of the soil, the orientation according to the sun, the degree of inclination, the covering of the soil, the history of the vegetation in the area…

In Rioja, density of the vegetation tends to vary a great deal. Older plantations, always en vaso, – the so-called 'bush-vines' –, harbour an average of some 3,500 vines per ha. More recent plantations contain up to 4,500 vines per ha. The yield then varying from 27 to 35 hl. per ha. land. No fertilisers of any kind are used: the wine is supposed to be an expression of the landscape itself. Fertilisers have plants turn lazy. Without them, roots go foraging as deeply as they can into the soil. Plants, furthermore, are left to grow any way they like, grass and weeds preventing erosion. They change into organic matter. Useful insects are given a chance to complete a natural life cycle. Not before the end of May does the vegetation get removed by hand. Weedkillers are an unknown notion in Roda.

The Roda team carefully monitors the maturing process of the grapes. The team is far more interested in the quality of the polyphenology than in alcohol and acidity percentages. It tests these resorting to tastings of the grapes' pips: laboratory research is taking place right now to make 'pip-tasting' a little more methodical. Roda delves far and deep when it comes to matters of research: another purely technical team contributes to a project to save the hundreds of existing Tempranillo clones. An experimental vineyard was created for the purpose.

As a rule, 12 different vintages from the 12 different Rioja Alta zones are produced after each harvest. The grapes do not arrive in a traditional container but in small plastic trays. These are in for examination and selection. Only the best are kept for later vinification. This selection table, and the presence of Fernando Remirez de Ganusa, were new in Rioja. The wine is macerated and given alcoholic fermentation in large, traditional, French oak barrels. Up to 45% is later stored in new French oak barrels, where it receives malolactic fermentation and continues to ripen over 18 to 24 months. Assembly takes place after 12 months. Repeated tastings determine which barrels are to head for Roda I and which for Roda II. The criteria used to differentiate between the two mainly involve longevity. Since both wines are outstanding in terms of balance and perfection and can be consumed when still quite young. Roda I tends to have more body and is mainly the wine of the future. The wines are never filtered before bottling, only slightly purified adding white of egg.
Another spectacular Roda-team project turned out to be the 'Cirsion', the idea of which goes back to 1994. On testing the vineyard grapes, the oenologists established differences in taste. A number of objective criteria were resorted to, to help determine the physiology of this occurrence. Vinification materialized for a first time in 1997. The product then was still kept off the market: there was really not enough to go round! Cirsion needed a maximum in fruit, stability in colour and as much mildness as possible. This included picking grapes with a high degree of polymerisation. Or, as they say at Roda's: those few grapes that have begun the wine processing on their own. In the year 2000 and for the very first time did the Cirsion 1998 safely reach the market. The result was clearly worthy of Roda. In a word: spectacular!

Cut into the rock is the cellar for storing the vats

The wine is transferred to other vats.

Roda advertising in Rioja-villages by means of a flyer.

VITICULTOR:

- **COMPRAMOS UVA TINTA DE VIÑAS DE MAS DE TREINTA AÑOS EN RIOJA ALTA**
- PAGOS AL CONTADO (24 HORAS)
- BUEN PRECIO
- NO IMPORTA QUE EL VOLUMEN DE LA PARTIDA SEA PEQUEÑO.
- POSIBILIDAD DE HACER CONTRATOS PARA VARIOS AÑOS.
- SISTEMA DE TRANSPORTE NEGOCIABLE, PODRIAMOS RETIRAR NOSOTROS LA UVA DE LA PARCELA.
- VOLUMEN DE COMPRAS LIMITADO.
- INTERESADOS LLAMAR AL

TELEFONO : 43 51 05

Range

3 red wines

Roda II, Reserva
Tempranillo (mostly from 70 to 80%) and Garnacha (mostly from 20 to 30%), planned for the future: Graciano
Dark red in colour with an agreeable nose of ripe black fruit; pleasantly spicy. Concentration and body, structure and finesse. Lingering aftertaste.

Roda I, Reserva
Tempranillo (mostly at the rate of 100% in Roda II years – and a small portion Garnacha produced during exclusively Roda I years; up to now: 1994 and 1997).
Deep red in colour, fairly tight nose opening up when swirled, intricate mix of red fruit, scalding, nicely balanced French oak. Very high concentration but also alluring and with a great deal of finesse. Pleasantly knotted tannins and acids making the wine immediately available for consumption, with assertive keeper qualities, most of all.

Cirsion
Tempranillo
A dark red-ink gown. Hugely intricate nose of mainly black fruit whilst maintaining the necessary fraîcheur. (A fruit tree for the palate), explosive fruit cocktail palate, velvet tannins like a bite in a ripe grape. Perfect maturity and balance. A strong and grand finale on velvet. Majestic.

Export

Main countries for export: the USA, Switzerland, Britain, Germany, Japan and Sweden.

PRODUCT OF SPAIN
RODA I
RESERVA
1996
BODEGAS RODA, S.A.
HARO - LA RIOJA
cl.e
RIOJA
DENOMINACIÓN DE ORIGEN

Finca Allende

Plaza Ibarra 1
Finca Allende
26330 Briones
Tel: 941 32 23 01
Fax: 941 32 23 02
E-mail: fallende@fer.es

Miguel Angel De Gregorio

Owners: Miguel Angel and Mercedes De Gregorio

Oenologist and agronomist: Miguel Angel De Gregorio

Surface: 22 ha. vineyards

Production: Allende: 170,000 bottles
(in future 300,000 bottles max.)
Aurus: 5 to 7,000 bottles

Type: red (in future: also white)

The Briones coat of arms, which is also depicted on the Allende label

Miguel Angel De Gregorio, a passionate whirlwind, terroir-obsessed

The man is like a whirlwind – so hard to pin down! Miguel Angel De Gregorio is so talented he can do anything and everything at once. He continually comes up with new ideas, new projects and new wine. To him, 36 hours in the day simply are not enough. When he talks, it's like a stream of words turning into a torrent. You only fully grasped his first argument when he already launched into another, with 5 telephone calls and 3 e-mails thrown in…
He is the walking encyclopedia of the Rioja in the renaissance-like sense of the word: a *Homo Universalis* of Rioja. Whatever happened in the area in the past, its people, its wine-producers, its vineyards: Miguel Angel knows about it all. An afternoon is his company does not necessarily mean it may end after two or three hours: you could leave at dusk, under the impression he told you only half of what he intended to say. It seems he is not satisfied with a single harvest. There could be a dozen harvests as far as he is concerned, one for each month of the year. For he personally will manage to produce new wine, and better, with each harvest. Miguel Angel's passion is wine. And so is the place he grew up in: Rioja.

He was only 6 months old when his family left far away Almodóvar del Campo in La Mancha. They settled in La Rioja where his father, Nicolás De Gregorio, found work managing one of Rioja's main wine-houses, the Marqués de Murrieta. The boy Miguel Angel played in the vast vineyards of Murrieta's 'Finca Ygay'; he also soon started helping with the pruning and lending a hand with the harvest. He grew up in the vineyards, amongst the wine-producers and their wine.

He never hesitated much about what he wanted to do and be in life: it revolved around wine. Miguel Angel trained as an agricultural engineer and is an oenologist. He qualified with flying colours and, at the age of 25, was appointed the manager and oenologist of Bodegas Bretón, a fairly small bodega in Logroño, the capital of the Rioja region. The bodega produced mainly classic Rioja wine types: a young white and a red wine, crianza's, reserva's and gran reserva's. Nothing really new under the sun.

The beautiful mansion in the village of Briones.

p. 118: One of the stops on the way of the cross, the 'Calvario'

p. 119: Beautiful view of the small village of Briones

In a matter of years, he had raised bodega Breton's standards; he was also given 'carte blanche' by the owner for a new project: Dominio de Conté, a wine originating in a single vineyard, alongside the Ebro riverbank in Briones. Miguel was then 30. In 1994 he put this wine's first millésime on the market, the millésime 1989. The wine was new for Rioja in spite of the restrictions of the moment.

Miguel Angel nevertheless intended to take things further. With the help of Mercedes, his sister, he began making his own wine in 1995. It was to be the start of the big 'wine-adventure'. He did not hesitate much as to the name: it was to be 'Allende', synonymous of 'mas allá', in Spanish. In free translation: 'always further towards the other side' or, in Miguel-language: 'citius, altius, fortius'.

Experimenting had already begun at an earlier stage, in fact: already by the mid-80's had he been given the opportunity to fully investigate various vineyards in Briones and try these out. The Oenology faculty of Madrid, where he was a lecturer, organized its practicals in Briones. He thereby thoroughly knew all the existing vineyards in and around the village; he also had started buying smaller vineyards here and there since 1986. By the time 1995 arrived, he was in no doubt as to where he would be heading for.

All this had been his own project, with no-one but Mercedes to rely on and help out; there had been no financial backing from anywhere. Miguel and Mercedes could not afford much: there was none too much ready cash to invest in real estate: any money they had went to buying vineyards. They then rented a microscopic bodega and give it the start off. Miguel was well aware of the quality of the grapes he had invested in, the standard of the barrels that were best French and another reason to be rightly proud: Miguel Angel seems to be alone in Spain (and alone outside Burgundy) to be allowed the purchase of such barrels by the famous 'François Frères', from the Domaine de la Romanée Conti's own tonnellerie. One soon discovers, pacing the vineyards with him, a genuine passion for all that is Bourgogne as much as for the Grand Cru terroirs.

In 1997 he put his first wine on the market, the Allende 1995. The wine was an instant success. It soon got noticed in the U.S.A. where its potential was applauded: Miguel Angel was in business.

Visit Briones and you may notice there are signs of its rich wine tradition everywhere. Over 600 bodega's are to be found in it! And way up are the 'cliff-s', hacked out of the rock formation itself. From the top of the cliffs you will see San Vincente de la Sonsierra, also

on a hillside and Briones' 'enemy' throughout history. San Vicente used to be part of Navarre: a border kapt the two villages separate. In the meantime both municipalities come under Rioja Alta – San Vicente bordering onto Rioja Alavesa with Briones as the last village but one in Rioja Alta.

Time did not stand still for Miguel Angel and his vineyards: he even acquired part of the 'Calvario', a hillside location of 12 ha. This was one of his best moves. In time, he will probably own the entire vineyard. The hill was named after a Way of the Cross leading to the top, – a true 'Calvary hill'! But Miguel Angel wants to see 12 micro-climate terroirs there some day, one for each Station of the Cross. He once again intends to proceed according to guidelines in Bourgogne, mostly the Côte de Nuits with its famous Grand Cru's. He also called one of his vineyards 'La Tarea' ('La Tâche' in French).

Miguel's is not for lowering standards. He is not the 'tonnellerie François Frères' privileged client in vain (and the third in importance – after Domaine de la Romanée Conti and Domaine Leroy). These names are references in themselves. Wine coming from the acquired barrels and currently in them, will appear on the market as 'Calvario'. Something to look forward to!

He always laughs when telling the story of his progress. Whenever he goes to France for instance, he takes a 'press file' with cuttings and clippings from the foreign press about his wine. The French being besotted with wine guru Parker he shows them his articles and how he never scored below the 90 mark in the famous Wine Advocate. It mostly does the trick!

Personally, we have another reason to believe in Miguel Angel: the sheer quality of his wine! With the Allende, a first from 100% Tempranillo in 1995, he also brought out the Aurus, in 1996.

The said Aurus is the bodega's pride and joy! It is 85% Tempranillo and 15% Graciano from very old vine stock. A first selection takes place on picking the grapes; another on the selection table when the grapes reach the bodega. No racemes are taken off their stems, in typi-

cal and traditional Rioja fashion. A 28 day maceration period follows. The wine then stays some 18 months on ⅓ new French (Tronçais) oak. Like the Allende, the Aurus reaches the market as a normal annual production, without being referred to as 'crianza' or 'reserva'. Miguel Angel does not care for traditional Rioja appellations much: he says they only cause confusion abroad and for people not really being used to them. He moreover wants to heed the wine itself before determining how long it stays to stay on wood, not some faceless rule on the matter…

There is to be an addition to Aurus and Calvario shortly in the form of a white 'Allende'; it will be of ancient Viura vines. It is sampling splendidly already now: the very proof of a great future in store.

Miguel Angel used all Briones had to offer in the way of geography and climate the best he could. He owes it to his estate to keep investigating further in his quest for renewal and innovation! A search taking him well outside Rioja already. He once returned to La Mancha for a closer look at own roots. And he started a wine there too! What more has this man in store for us?

Range

2 red wines
Allende
100% Tempranillo
12 months on mainly French oak
Deep red in colour. Very expressive red fruit nose with lots of fraîcheur and obvious spiciness. Very savoury palate, fruity, nicely balanced, equally distributed acids. A goodly structure and a beautiful finale.

Aurus
85% Tempranillo, 15% Graciano
18 months French oak
Very dark ink in colour when poured out. Densely concentrated nose opening up slowly, lots of black fruit, liquorice, herbs and attractive hints of minerals, scalding, cocoa and mint. Very dense palate, an explosion of fruits with a great deal of sophistication and body. Bordering onto the overripe. Nicely mature and lithe tannin structure. Full and harmonius. Very lengthy aftertaste. A little terroir-bitterness in the finale.

Calvario (for the future)
almost 100% Tempranillo
12 to 18 months French oak
Dark yellow in colour. Appealing mineral nose with lots of black fruit, if mainly plums and candied black forest fruits. The nose has a nice touch of leather and contains beautiful wood. Powerful start-off, but lithe body with plenty of attractive ripe tannins. Very full and harmonious. Well balanced with a long finale. Native tang.

Export

70% outside Spain, mainly Germany, Britain, Japan, the U.S.A. and Switzerland

ALLENDE
1997
PRODUCIDO Y EMBOTELLADO POR:
FINCA ALLENDE S.L.
SAN ASENSIO - RIOJA - ESPAÑA
R.E.N.º 4 - LR
RIOJA
DENOMINACION DE ORIGEN CALIFICADA
75 cl.13% vol.
N º 04569

Señorío de Otazu

31174 Echauri
SEÑORÍO DE OTAZU
Tel.: 948 32 92 00
Fax: 948 32 93 53
E-mail: otazu@mx3.redestb.es

Owners: S.A. Gabarbide

Manager: Pedro Bañales

Oenologist: Javier Colio

Agronomist: Pedro Bañales – Carlos Chocarro

Surface: 350 ha., including 110 ha. vineyard

Production: 650,000 bottles

Type: white and red

Pedro Bañales

The impressively renovated 'Palacio de Otazu'

Impressive to start off with

This is one of the most impressive estates I ever saw. The bodega has been registered part of DO Navarra since 1994. Until the DO, in 1958, there had not been the slightest vinicultural activity in the area anymore. Vines had simply vanished...

For this is the Otazu, not so obviously wine-producing country, located as it is to the extreme North of Navarre, in the Pamplona cuenca, 8 kms from the town. In the distance you see the imposing mass of sierras El Perdón and La Peña de Echauri. This is Spain's red wine country that is geographically furthest North of all.

After the phylloxera, no-one bothered to plant vines any more here. The vine-pest hit Navarre worst of all: some 99% of vineyards had gone down with it. The area had been quite a famous appellation in the past; for the present-day, DO registered, 13,945 ha. still represent only a quarter of the 1891 figure.

Navarre once owned the oldest commercial vineyard on record, in Funes, on the river Arga. It was laid on by the Romans in the 2nd century B.C., as army food supplies. The name Navarre also comes from the Romans. Vineyards thrived during the Middle-Ages: Navarre was on the pilgrimage route to Santiago de Compostela. Olite and Puenta la Reina being the better known stop-overs. Up to this day, Olite remains famous as a centre for wine. Production went increasing all over Navarre then, also in Moorish times.

Navarre's wine culture of the past may well be connected to French roots in history. It had been part of that country until 1512, since the crowning of the king of Navarre, Theobald II, in 1234.

But Ferdinando 'el Católico' took over all land South of the Pyrenees in 1512 and was the first King of Unified Hiberia. The French did not let go easily: only in 1791 did Louis XVI

The old bodega that has been completely restored.

French oak vats of Allier lie maturing in the impressive maturation cellar.

resign his title as ' Roi de France et de Navarre'. By then, Navarre really had turned into a part of Spain.

Navarre had always been one of the more prosperous countries South of the Pyrenees. It had a lot of cattle, grain, and – of course – there was the wine. So famous towards the end of the 19th century it turned out the area's main agricultural resource. Bordeaux also played a role in this. Many French wine-producers headed for Spain to secure some supplies after the oïdium plague at home. Navarre stayed a favourite destination owing to its own tradition in wine and because it was closest to Bordeaux.

At that time, there already was a lot of activity where the bodega stands now. The phylloxera died out, running short of plants to feed on. Otazu lay neglected until the arrival of its new owners (and that was quite recent). These new owners officially acquired Otazu and Eriete in 1989.

Two estates are involved here: the Señorío (literally: a domain or manor) de Eriete and the Señorío de Otazu. They also border onto one another. Until 1956, the Señorío de Eriete used to belong to the aristocratic Mora y Aragón branch, the family of Queen Fabiola of Belgium. Señorío de Otazu had been the property of the Marqués de Echandía until 1941. Both estates were sold at the same time, to the 'Semillas Ebro S.A.' company. They were resold in 1989, this time to the current owners.

These owners planned a bright future for their estate! They appointed a manager, Pedro Bañales and, from 1992 to 1994, kept on refurbishing their vineyards, replanting as much as they could where grapes had grown all those centuries ago.

In fact, the estate has two very splendid mansions and one bodega. One of the mansions, the Palacio de Otazu, was entirely restored to its former glory and is the pride of the district. The Palacio de Eriete lies a little further and is also in for renovation soon.

All, nevertheless happens in and around the bodega! The more ancient construction, dating back

The 'Palacio de Otazu' – the impressive bodega

These amphoras have mainly served as decoration since the introduction of cuves inox.

Persistent stories will have us believe that Napoleon's armies were encamped here...

to 1860, was entirely renovated and the old equipment taken out. A new bodega was fitted into former premises (a vast wine-ripening cellar included). The new architecture is unique! The bodega's historic parts have been connected to the cellars. The first wine-cellar with its 14 casks is under the mansion itself. Another reminder of this house's ties with wine history!

Pedro shows us around in the huge cellar space: the old wine cellar leads to a large and modern dining room completely out of glass to one side; hyper-modern kitchens with every facility are to the other. The vast window looks out onto the new cellar, a giant construction with vaulted arches in concrete, superbly reflecting the light. The wine can be seen ripening in its French oak barrels, from both the tasting room and the dining room.

Back to ground-floor level, you will find two hobs, one to each side of the former bodega. The new bodega's architectural input, with its glass, steel, wood and concrete perfectly integrates into the historic whole. The modern bodega has new casks, all of these inox.

The vineyards surround the bodega: traditional Tempranillo, and – owing to the climate and historic links with France – much Cabernet Sauvignon, red Merlot and red Chardonnay. Originally, there were 5 different clones of each red wine vine, the grapes to be separately vinified later. Results could be individually analysed this way. The Chardonnay came in 3 different clones.

A Chardonnay harvest always takes place at night to avoid any scorching temperatures. Thus counteracting oxidation and safeguarding acids. Nights can be pretty cold in these Northern parts, the temperature dropping sharply in comparison to the heat of the day.

The red wine is given a traditional ripening on French Allier oak; 1/3 of all barrels is new; the oldest are 4 years old. The white wine (Chardonnay) comes from two different vinifications: a Chardonnay without wood, presenting all the facets taken on by this grape and another Chardonnay, fermented on new French oak and a limited layering on the same oak. Fruit and grapes always staying predominant in the taste.

A first Reserva red wine was recently brought out. Most of the vines being far too young at this stage, no oenologist is going to venture making top-wines with these. They may nevertheless be clearly in the offing. All the necessary elements are more than definitely present to have the estate play a leading role onto the wine scene of Navarre. Its owners furthermore like quality, not quantity! This is also why they managed reviving this countryside's (particularly their own valley's) glorious tradition.

The DO Navarra perfectly understood what was happening: it reintegrated the district into the appellation it had once been part of, if a century ago.

Range

3 red wines

Palacio de Eriete, crianza
Tempranillo, Merlot, Cabernet Sauvignon
12 months French oak
Bright red in colour. Lovely nose with red fruit, leather, delicate touches of wood. The fruitiness returns to the palate; goodly acids and well balanced tannins. Neat aftertaste.

Palacio de Otazu, Crianza
15% Tempranillo, 40% Merlot, 45% Cabernet Sauvignon
12 months French oak
Bright red. The nose has a red paprika and pepper piquant, its spiciness turning into fruitiness: redcurrant, forest fruits; smooth leather and coffee-like hints to the background. Nicely balanced in the mouth with lots of fruit and stable tannins. Beautiful finale.

Palacio de Otazu, Reserva
60% Cabernet Sauvignon, 30% Merlot, 10% Tempranillo
12 months French oak
Bright red and mirror-like. Nose predominantly Cabernet; paprika's, black fruit, mint and touches of leather. A palate with a powerful start-off, settling towards the middle. Nice fruitiness. Drawn out finale.

3 white wines

Palacio de Eriete Chardonnay
100% Chardonnay
Bright red in colour. Lovely Chardonnay nose, with dabs of cream and exotic fruits. Very pure also in the mouth. Well balanced, lots of fraîcheur. Sophisticated finale.

Palacio de Otazu, Chardonnay
100% Chardonnay
Bright red in colour. An explosion of exotic fruits in its nose, citrus, discrete dabbing of milk. A pleasant palate with lots of steady acids. Neat aftertaste.

Palacio de Otazu,Chardonnay fermentado en barrica
100% Chardonnay
Fermentation and a 6 months layering on new French oak
A golden gown. Orange and grapefruity nose initially, throwing in exotic fruit and bits of butter later, toasted bread, almonds. Full start-off, the right wood-fruit balance. Not too pompous, staying gracious. Full aftertaste ending into a pleasant 'bitter'. Lots of added fraîcheur.

Bodega Otazu
Bodega Otazu
Product of Spain
Palacio
de
OTAZU
NAVARR
DENOMINACION DE ORIGEN
RED WINE
CRIANZA 1996
Bodega del Señorío de Otazu
Gabarbide S.A. - Echauri - Navarra
EMBOTELLADO EN ORIGEN - ESTATE BOTTLED
750 ml e

Hermanos Pérez Pascuas

Ctra. de Roa
HERMANOS PÉREZ PASCUAS
09314 Pedrosa de Duero
Tel.: 947 53 01 00
Fax: 947 53 00 02

Manuel, Adolfo, Benjamin and José-Manuel Pérez with a portrait of the founder Mauro Pérez, in the background

Owners: the Pérez Pascuaso brothers

Oenologist: José-Manuel Ruiz

Agronomist: José-Manuel Pérez

Area: 100 ha.

Production: 400,000 bottles

Type: Red

The name of the wine is proudly displayed on the facade of the new bodega.

Family tradition and innovation in Ribera del Duero

This bodega is an example of tradition for this appellation, but at the same time forms part of one of the most modern and progressive wines of the region. The three brothers, Benjamin, Manuel and Adolfo run this family business together, with an emphasis on quality.
Father Mauro Perez planted his vines during the 40s and 50s. At that time he already owned 35 ha. of vineyards and was therefore one of the village's biggest owners. However, the grapes that were harvested here were mainly sent to the local cooperative. At that time Ribera del Duero was not an appellation, and the region only acquired DO status in 1982. There were very few bodegas that operated independently. The main activity lay in those bodegas that were to be found in most villages. It was on the incentive of the three Perez brothers in 1982 that the decision was made to make their own wine. At that time there were not even 10 operative bodegas to be found in the entire region of Ribera. The first Vina Pedrosa was created in a small bodega in Pedrosa itself. This wine soon became known as an example of quality all over Spain.
However, the breakthrough for these wines both in Spain and abroad took place after the arrival of José Manuel Pérez, son of Benjamin and representative of the youngest generation of the family. José-Manuel was a young idealistic oenologist who fully supported his father's concept of quality. From 1989 José-Manuel started working as an oenologist in the family bodega. Whereas before 1989 the wines had had a certain rustic character, this now changed. Elegance and finesse are key words for José Manuel. Like Carles Pastrana in the Priorat, José Manuel managed to make gems of elegance and finesse using the power and the material present in his grapes. Not only was there an improvement in the style of the wines from 1989, indeed an additional bodega was built just outside the village, bordering in the west on the outer boundaries of the vineyards of the appellation and on the silhouette of the Sierra de Guadarrama in the south. The new bodega was built against a hill as it were, so that the actual maturing cellar could be made underground. Situated above this cellar was a pine forest that protected the cellar from too much heat from the sun. During the summer this pine forest is sprayed with water every day in order to keep the underground cool.

Pérez Pascuas is the owner of one of the oldest vineyards of the Ribera del Duero.

The new bodega was built in Catalan style in 1989.

The pride and joy of the Pérez Pascuas family: the vat cellar; without a doubt it is one of the most impressive cellars in Spain.

Once more this illustrates yet another unmistakable characteristic of the Pérez Pascuas family: perfectionism in every detail ranging from the vine, to the maturing, and on to the bottling and transport to the client.

A dining table is placed on the edge of the pine forest in the pleasant company of the Pérez Pascuas brothers. With bread rubbed in with olive oil and Jamón Serrano, lomo, chorizo and queso manchego, I experienced one of the most memorable picnics of my life, especially with a Vino Pedrosa Gran reserva 1992 for company, which changed the meal into a veritable feast. In this domain there is a simplicity and modesty that has continued in spite of the creation of one of the most complex and complete wines on the Iberian peninsula.

After the bodega had been built the quality and its attendant fame rapidly grew. The total area of vineyards increased to almost 100 ha. More than half of this consisted of vines more than 25 years old which was fairly exceptional in this appellation. José-Manuel becomes thoughtful whenever there is mention of the many bodegas that are sprouting up all over the area. Every new visit reveals additional new buildings along the roadside, each even grander than the next. These are mainly the work of investors from Madrid who are keen to profit from the reputation of this fashionable appellation and make a quick return. However, fast financial returns and the making of quality wine profit do not go well together. Because these houses often do not have a vineyard or only have very young plants, they often buy their grapes from the cooperatives, thereby creating scarcity and a quick rise in prices.

Things even reached a point where this type of 'investment wines' were going for the same price (or were even more expensive), as the wines made by serious wine makers like Pérez Pascuas. However, the lavish harvest of 1999 will ensure that the cash register will sound far less frequently at these 'parvenu domains'; indeed production has increased fivefold. An amount that is impossible to sell at existing high prices. The only survivors in this boom will be serious bodegas.

In order to achieve this quality the wine makers of Pérez Pascuas frequently have to be merciless; it is necessary to be highly selective and often half the grapes are not harvested because they do not meet quality standards. In some years (such as 1993), no wine was even brought out. In this case, the yield per vine is then only just 1 to 1.5 kg, or not quite 20 hl/ha. The vineyards consist mainly of Tinto Fino, as the Tempranillo is called in Ribera del Duero, but 10% of the production also consists of Cabernet Sauvignon. The Cabernet Sauvignon grapes are mainly used for the Reservas and the Gran Reservas to give them a little more structure and a long life. Until recently mainly American oak was used for the crianza. The Tempranillo of Pérez Pascuas combines very well with the American wood. During my last visit however, I was struck by the increase in the stock of French oak vats. Whereas this had so far been mainly used for the Cabernet Sauvignon and the Gran

Along the road from Roa de Duero to Pedrosa de Duero are the well-kept vineyards of the Viña Pedrosa.

One of the 'Tinta del Pais' vines of the old 'Pago de Valtoneña' vineyard – it was here that the grapes were harvested for the unrivalled Pérez Pascuas Gran Selección.

A large section of the collection of vats consist of American oak, but recently more and more French oak is being used.

The Cabernet Sauvignon vines have been planted 'en espaldena'.

Seleccion, more French oak was now being used for the other wines as well. In his wines, it is increasingly evident that José Manuel is searching for greater finesse.
José Manuel is an artist when it comes to combining finesse and strength. Although these wines are ready for consumption they nevertheless have an enormous potential for the future. For instance only now is the Pérez Pascuas Gran Selección 1991 beginning to show itself fully, and this is after a period of 9 years! One house in this region achieves the same result with regard to the long life of older vintages: Vega Sicilia – but then they are the pioneers of this style.
This Pérez Pascuas Gran Selección is a wine that is only made in top years (such as '91 and '94). This is a wine that is made from vines that are more than 50 years old, and originate from one Pago de Valtarrena vineyard. The name 'Gran Selección' must be taken quite literally: the vats of wine from this vineyard are tasted many times. For every tasting, only those vats that have the best results are kept. In the end there is only very little left of the 12,000 l that is harvested. Only 5,000 to 6,000 bottles are distributed worldwide amongst the different distributors.
However, let us not put the other wines in the shade: they too are all top wines; unsurprisingly, the crianza, the reserva and the gran reserva are among the best wines to be found on the Spanish market. The quality standards are also extremely high for these wines. A preselection is made at the beginning of September in which the less ripe bunches of grapes are removed. The harvest takes place late in the season in order to get as much polyphenols as possible. Macerations usually last for a month and the malolactic fermentation occurs on the oak vats. No vat is older than three years. The crianza for example remains for 12 months on new oak and then for 6 months on second year oak. Nevertheless the crianza wines are fruit bombs which do need a bit of time, but in which there is a perfect integration of fruit and wood. The tannins are emphatically present but fine and mild. Strength and smoothness in harmony is one of the key concepts in understanding the wines of Pérez Pascuas. José Manuel is one of the wine artists who in the manner of the perfectionist, is busy with his work day in day out, without seeking the limelight in any way. This modesty becomes him, for without a doubt he makes one of the very best wines in Spain and in the world.

Range

4 red wines

Viña Pedrosa Crianza
100% Tinto fino
18 months on American oak, of which ⅔ new
Dark red in colour. A very pleasant nose, ripe blackberries, bilberries, black currants, mineral, leather, furred game, toasted vanilla. Juicy onset with a wide midriff. Full and fruity. A lot of acids in balance with smooth tannins. Elegant towards the end. Complex finale. Good taste.

Viña Pedrosa Reserva
90% Tinto fino, 10% Cabernet Sauvignon
24 months on American and French oak
Very dark red colour. Also a highly complex nose of black fruit, black currant, coffee, chocoate, minerals and a hint of toast with vanilla, furred game. Forceful onset with plenty of fruit. Packs of fruit, beautifully structured with tannins and acids. Broad in the mouth. A wine of the future. Great finesse and an enormous length.

Viña Pedrosa Gran Reserva
90% Tinto fino, 10% Cabernet Sauvignon
26 months on American and French oak
Dark red reflection. Masterful nose of Tinto Fino: elegant black fruit, coffee, leather, vanilla and furred game, almost animal. Smooth onset and powerful midriff with plenty of fruit. Very young in the mouth with a lot of acids and juicy tannins. Juicy towards the finale. Sexy finale full of elegance. A great wine.

Pérez Pascuas Gran Selección
100% Tinto fino
26 months on French oak
Ink-black colour. A nose that does not open easily, very closed. After breathing for a long period of time, very fine and elegant fruit tones, toasted vanilla, black forest fruits, minerals. Very fine onset in the mouth with an enormous amount of dominated power. Marvellous structure, balanced use of wood, acids and tannins. A monument to finesse. Very long finale that makes you want more. Addictively tasty.

Export

40% of the production distributed over 35 countries

Pérez Pascuas
RIBERA DEL DUERO
Denominación de Origen
Pérez Pascuas
Esta "Gran Selección"
consta de 5.880 botellas
Nº 000935
GRAN RESERVA
1994
Bodegas Hnos. Pérez Pascuas, S.L.
Pedrosa de Duero (Burgos) España
75 cl.
PRODUCT OF SPAIN
13% Vol.

Bodegas Reyes

Ctra de Valladolid
BODEGAS REYES
47300 Peñafiel
Tel.: 983 87 30 15
Fax: 983 87 30 17

Teófilo Reyes

Owners: Juanjo and Luis Reyes

Oenologist: Teófilo Reyes

Agronomist: Teófilo Reyes

Surface: 60 ha.

Production: 250,000 bottles

Type: red

Teófilo Reyes, Ribera del Duero's living memory

Teófilo is a living legend in Ribera del Duero and in the whole of Spain. He is the founder of the appellation, in fact. Before his appearance on the scene, the area (no appellation until 1982) had mainly been a producer of rosé and light red wines (the so-called ' claretes'), but for the Vega Sicilia, naturally! The arrival and the insight of Teófilo would considerably alter the style and the reputation of the region altogether.
Born in 1922, in La Horra, he was already strongly attracted by the world of wine at quite an early age. In 1946, he beheld his first degree in chemistry from the University of Salamanca. 2 years later, he rounded up his studies with another degree in 'capataz & viticultura y enología' from the Haro Oenologic Institute, where he had been the head laureate. His worshipped Haro teacher was Don Antonio Larrea, a famous Spanish oenologist at that time. Larrea would be appointed chairman DOC Rioja later on; he asked Teófilo to lecture in oenology in Logroño. Teófilo Reyes also taught physics and chemistry at the Aranda de Duero Institute until his retirement in 1987. He had been an inspired and enthusiastic pedagogue for over 30 years and formed several generations of oenologists and scientists with his teachings.

In the world of wine itself, the baptism of fire only really came in 1950, when he managed to gather 18 La Horra wine-growers into one of the region's first modern bodega's: Santa Eulalia. Setting up the bodega was more than simply welcome for the development of the wine growing activities in the area. It represented a pilot project in cooperation that would be copied over and over again and engender bodega's for 20 years to come. Something Teófilo himself considered very important. His interests went beyond 'Santa Eulalia': he was involved in the setting up and the daily running of bodega's Anguix (1956), Olmedillo (1959), Nava de Roa (1960) and Fuentecén (1962). They all were engaged in the production of 'claretes'.

Two crucial events took place in 1954 en 1974. In 1954 Teófilo assumed the leadership of the technical side of bodega 'Ribera Duero', as it was known at the time, in Peñafiel. It is

The beautiful Castillo de Peñafiel overlooks the Duero valley. A modern museum of winegrowing has been established here since 2000.

called 'Protos' today. The bodega had been fairly important for the region until 1940. It had fallen upon hard times later. Teofilo managed to put it back on its tracks after the 1954 harvest. 'Protos' thrived, even though the necessary means were not always available. In 1970, a first underground storage-place was created as a result, delving into the rock on top of which stands the famous castle of Peñafiel. Teófilo was in 'Protos' until 1972. The bodega owes its current fame to the successes of that man's pioneering days.

In 1974, Teófilo made the acquaintance of Alejandro and Federico Fernández. These two brothers owned a mechanic's workshop in Pesquera de Duero but wanted to start a bodega.

A delicate operation, both technically and financially; and one that involved making headway using such tools as happened to be available often no more than some old shed and open air fermentation vessels. But an unlikely adventure had begun. The 'Pesquera' wine started here. A huge success for Teófilo Reyes and Alejandro Fernández at home but also, and mainly, in countries abroad. In 1982, Teófilo managed to convince Alejandro Fernández to invest more in technical equipment. Ribera del Duero had just been granted a DO-status and investments were to be turn out fully lucrative soon. An horizontal press and the necessary 'inox' barrels were bought. Teófilo Reyes was to create the wine of a lifetime in that place! His skills in the field of oenology were applauded everywhere in Spain and abroad. The bodega (and its owners) blossomed.

For 20 years, Teofilo had been dedicated, heart and soul, to the Pesquera-project; when Alejandro Fernández suddenly shut him out. All the celebrated oenologist had left was this long-time experience at the top of the Spanish wine world. When Teófilo relates this part of his life's story he still tends to get emotional. So might anyone who had to start all over again at the age of 72…

It was then Juanjo and Luis Reyes – Teófilo's sons – managed to persuade their father to indeed start afresh, whatever the odds. This time however, his precious and extensive know-how would not get used and abused by strangers. Juanjo and Luis' project reached

further: they would set up an own bodega in honour of their father. And father would soon prove the mark of respect had been in no way been misplaced. In 1994, bodega Reyes was taking off, with very few means and as little as 2.5 ha. of vineyard space. But, no-one in Ribera knew the local vineyards better than Teófilo. Was he not selecting grapes for the local wine-producers in 1950 already? All the knowledge acquired at the time was to be recycled to the full in the making of his own wine. The grapes he chose for his first millésime, the Teófilo Reyes Crianza 1994, would quickly yield results. As soon as it appeared on the market, the wine was viewed as some kind of a cult-wine, from the very hands of a living legend. It was the only Spanish wine the American wine magazine, the 'Wine Spectator', put on the list of the world's 10 best. With positive results: a few years later, Teófilo's new wine was given the status his former brainchild, the 'Pesquera' had received, and taken two decades to obtain. The move made by Juanjo and Luis in 1994 had certainly not been in vain!

Today, the bodega owns over 50 ha. of vineyard surface. Its plantations are recent, as maybe: it means a few more grapes will be in for selection by Teófilo, later. But the year 2000 will mark the triumph of this man of 78, who managed a remarkable achievement in a very short period. And new investments in the vineyards and the bodega indicate this is but the start of a bright new adventure!

From the technical point of view all is, indeed, fully up to date in the bodega. Teófilo knows every step of his wine-making and will explain the slightest chemical processes in every possible detail. Today, the bodega owns 1,100 American oak barrels, a large part of which are new. The new oak percentage increasing with the growth of the bodega itself. Production currently stands at 250,000 bottles. In the longer term it ought to climb to the 400,000 figure. It seems that, everywhere in the world, production can be considered sold in advance.

The wine made here is 'special': it is the most tempting, seductive, and succulent Ribera del Duero I ever tasted. Always tops (certainly in good years), but also in lesser years, like 1997. The hand of the master is there and stays omnipresent. A first Reserva was brought out, recently. This 1996 vintage will only come in magnums. Whereby it definitely ranks amongst keeper wines by excellence.

When I think that, in 1975, a famous Spanish oenologist (at a very high level within the official organisms of the Spanish wine world, at that!) forecast, smirking, Teófilo's projects and intentions (it involved the Tinto Fino) as to a grand red keeper from Ribera del Duero were doomed to fail (Ribera's grapes would not have had enough class of their own to turn into grand wines...) Fortunately for us, and for Ribera del Duero: Teófilo was stubborn and went ahead. He is jointly responsible for the hot spot this appellation turned into on the Spanish wine chart. Hurray for the man, I say. And may he fully enjoy his delightful wines for a very long time to come!

1994: The start of a new legend in Ribera del Duero

More than 50 ha. of vineyards have been planted in for future wines.

Range

2 red wines

Teófilo Reyes crianza
98% Tinto Fino, 2% Albillo
14 months on American oak
Dark red in colour. Savoury nose of black fruit, cocoa, wild fleecy game, pleasant touches of vanilla. Lots of 'fraîcheur' from the very start. Mellow tannins, nicely fruity. Inviting, very full-bodied, well balanced. Pleasant and lengthy finale.

Teófilo Reyes Reserva
98% Tinto Fino, 2% Albillo
20 months on American oak
Dark red in colour. Another succulent and fruity nose, if slightly more severe, mint and coffee-like overtones. Needs time. Masses of black fruit in the mouth, a balanced structure, nicely acid. Lovely ripe tannins, nevertheless. Drawn out aftertaste. A grandee.

Export

The production largely goes abroad, mainly to the USA, Britain, Germany and Japan.

BODEGAS REYES
RIBERA DEL DUERO
DENOMINACION DE ORIGEN
TEÓFILO REYES
TINTO CRIANZA
1997
PEÑAFIEL (VALLADOLID) · ESPAÑA
R.E. 7583 - VA

Mauro

Cervantes 12
BODEGAS MAURO
47320 Tudela de Duero
Tel.: 983 52 19 72
Fax: 983 52 19 73
E-mail: b-mauro@proinnet.com

Mariano García

Owner: Mauro S.A.

General manager: Mariano García Fernández

Business manager: Fernando Cabezudo San José

Oenologist: Isaac Fernández and Mariano García

Agronomist: José Barbero and Mariano García

Area: 35 ha. in Valladolid and 30 ha. in Toro

Production: 150,000 bottles

Type: red

The very best wines are made behind the discreet facade in the Calle Cervantes.

The birth of a 'Super-Duero'

Mariano García had already been the oenologist of the famous Spanish domain Vega Sicilia since 1968. Nevertheless, he dreamed of being absolutely free to have his own project with his own wines. Things came to a head in 1980 and Mauro was founded in Tudela de Duero. Because he was still the oenologist with Vega Sicilia (and continued to be so for many years to come), the bodega was initially run by his friends and partners, Luciano Suarez and Félix Coque. The start was very discreet: a small artisanal bodega in 'el Callejón del Boquerón' (the anchovy alley) was used for the first harvests up to 1985. The first harvests were very minimal: barely 5 to 10 thousand bottles left the bodega. Nevertheless these few bottles enjoyed success right from the very start, both in Spain itself as well as abroad. This was not surprising: a mini project with the Vega Sicilia oenologist as the initiator was still regarded with Argus' eyes.

Between 1980 and 1985 a start was made with the purchase of other vineyards. Besides old vines these also had newly planted vines and were located in the boroughs of Tudela de Duero and Santibáñez de Valcorba. Another important event took place in 1985 involving the purchase of an old 17th century town house in the centre of Tudela de Duero. The house was completely renovated and equipped for the making and storage of wine. With excellent results. Anyone who sees the very discreet facade from the outside will only see the small copper plate bearing the inscription 'Bodegas Mauro'. However, behind this facade lies the world of one of Spain's very best wines. This discretion is typical of this house; the work here is carried out seriously and precisely without there being a need to tell everyone about it. A positive feature that expresses great class and character.

The bodega gradually expanded and in 1991, 11 years later, production had risen to 60,000 bottles; a steady but not explosive growth. The main principle of the house is the quality and character of the wine, not quantity. Moreover, the quality improved each year. In Mariano García's view this was because both the vineyards and the people working them were acquiring more maturity. In 1994 Mariano's sons Eduardo and Mauro Alberto, joined the bodega. Mauro Alberto studied oenology in Blanquefort and underwent

The vineyards of Mauro enjoy a very special microclimate.

Young and old help with the harvest.

further training at the Bordeaux oenology department.
Although there was no doubt that the wines belonged to a select circle of the best wines in the regions, Mauro was not included in the appellation Ribera del Duero. Indeed in 1982 this appellation had been made too large to preserve a uniform character – when creating an appellation the main aim is to give each province its share of the appellation – but nobody thought to include the boroughs of Tudela de Duero and Santibáñez de Valcorba. Nevertheless, this would have been a nice reference for this young appellation. Indeed, the two villages have sufficient historical credentials to prove that this has always been a wine growing area.
Philip II even went so far as to exempt Tudela from having to pay taxes because of the quality of the grapes harvested there. Moreover, historical documents show that in 1785 Tudela, which was then very small, produced more than 3 million litres of wine. Not such a small wine area after all… In addition to this, Mauro owns 3 ha. in Tudela that are more than 50 years old.
All this has never upset Mariano García in any way. On the contrary, the situation has in fact given him more freedom to work according to his own principles. His wines do not need a DO's label as a quality guarantee for what is in the bottle. The name 'Mauro' is a

guarantee in itself. Mariano does not want to work under the restrictions of crianza and reserva, which in his view are restrictive for both the wines and the winegrower. There are oenologists who slavishly subject themselves to these standards without allowing the wine to speak. In Mauro it is the wine that determines how long it stays on the oak and when it is ready to be put onto the market. The parameters that are important in determining the life of the wine are the terroir, the selection of grapes and the characteristics of the harvest year, and not some written DO rule or other.

Nevertheless, strictly speaking, geographically and climatically the wines belong more to the Ribera del Duero than many others that fall within the DO. Until recently however, the wines have always been classified as 'Vinos de mesa' – table-wines – with the poor connotations that this has for an ignorant general public. With the creation of the 'Indicación Geográfica Protegida' (the IGT in Italy is the IGP in Spain), 'Vinos de la Tierra de Castilla y León', the future bottles of Mauro wines can be bottled under the label 'Vino de la Tierra'. Mariano prefers the name 'Super-Duero', which refers by analogy to the Super Tuscans, which usually falls outside the Italian DOCG and yet is superior in quality. There is nothing wrong with this approach, and it is certainly not plagiarism. If there is one wine that deserves this name, then it is that of Mauro.

The Mauro vineyards are subject to strongly fluctuating climatic conditions. Situated at a height of between 700 and 750 metres, it is very cold in winter (with an average temperature of 4 °C) and hot in the summer (average temperature 20 °C). The vineyards Mariano owns in Santibanez de Valcorba consist mainly of lime hills where the temperatures are even more extreme because this is where the highest vineyards are situated. The typical Ribera del Duero variety is mainly used here: Tinto Fino or Tempranillo. Besides this, the ordinary Mauro consists of 5% Syrah. This species of grape was planted 12 years ago as a supplement to the Tinto Fino in the Vinedo de Carramontemayor. Mariano is a great

The top wine of the house lies maturing in the very deepest cellar: the Terreus.

believer in this type of grape which give his wines a more Mediterranean character. Five years ago there were new plantings of 3.5 ha. new Syrah. A small percentage of Garnacha is used in the Vendimia Seleccionada, which is a type of grape that is very much used throughout Spain and which gives this wine a certain complexity, fruitiness and juiciness. The yields vary between 25 hl/ha. for vines that are more than 70 years old (Vina de Cueva Baja – the vineyard of the 'Terreus') to a maximum of 38 hl/ha. for more recent plantings (Vina de la Oliva, Vina del Esparragal and Vinedo de Carramontemayor). French oak is mostly used for the maturing of the different wines, as well as some American oak. This is generally used for the second year's maturing of the Vendimia Seleccionada after this has been matured on new French oak during the first year. Part of the wine – especially the Terreus – also has its malolactic fermentation in the oak vat. Moreover, Terreus is the darling and the showpiece of the domain: from 3 ha. of old vineyards that are more than 70 years old no more than about 6,000 bottles of this super concentrated fruit bomb are made. Nevertheless the wine is unbelievably fine and reflects the complex character of the Tinto Fino.
Not only the Terreus but also the 2 other wines from this domain are highly impressive and reflect Mariano García's knowhow. This passionate expertise was mainly acquired during the many years that he worked for Vega Sicilia. For thirty years, from 1968 to 1998, he was the oenologist for this historical wine domain. It was under his management that the style of this house was adapted to the modern age and the maturing period of most wines was shortened. In 1991 he created the Alion, another marvellous wine inspired by Vega Sicilia – the bodega is situated further away towards Penafiel. However, he has not been associated with this domain since 1998, and is completely free to work on 'his' Mauro wine.
It is very typical of him however, that he continues to search for new challenges: in 1994 he started doing micro-vinifications with grapes from Toro which lies more to the west. In 1996 he even bought vineyards in this region, and his first Toro wine, the San Roman, was made in 1997. This first vintage did not yet fall under the DO Toro because the wine was vinified on the Mauro domain in Tudela. However the wine fell under the DO Toro as from 1998, and by then the vineyards had already been extended to 30 ha. In 2000 the wine was even being made in the bodega at San Roman de Hornija. When a man like Mariano Garcia starts to buy vineyards in another region this soon becomes common knowledge and in the two years following the purchase of the vineyards, other wine makers who had followed Mariano in his search for quality in Toro, made unbelievably large investments. Other large projects are those of Vega Sicilia and of Alejandro Fernandez.
An ambitious project was started in the DO Ribera del Duero itself: together with Javier Zacagnini he founded Bodegas Aalto in 1999: this too was a domain with big plans for the future. However the thread that runs through all Mariano's wines is quality, and especially the perfect balance between strength and elegance. There are very few oenologists who master this art as perfectly as he does. It is undoubtedly thanks to the vision of oenologists like Mariano Garcia that Spain has become the hot spot on the winelists of the world.

The harvest in Toro for the San Romain 2000 is done using small bins.

M.

Range

3 red wines

Mauro
95% Tinto fino, 5% Syrah
11 to 14 months mainly French oak (70%), of which ⅓ is new
Dark red in colour. In the nose touches of black fruit, liquorice, chocolate, mint, torrefaction and minerals. Powerful onset, but smooth, balanced, ripe tannins with beautiful black fruit. Perfectly balanced with the acids. Very long aftertaste and elegant finale.

Mauro Vendimia Seleccionada
97% Tinto Fino, 3% Garnacha
24 months, of which 12 months in new French oak and 12 months in American oak
Almost ink-coloured. Once again touches in the nose of black fruit, cocoa, cherries, plums, fig paste, beautiful mineral tones, liquorice, and a hint of wood. Very concentrated onset, superbly balanced: fruit, acids, tannins: everything is smooth and yet powerful at the same time. Strong flavour of black fruit in the mouth. Very juicy and pleasant but at the same time extremely complex. Terroir wine. Very long finale. Top quality.

Terreus
100% Tinto fino
14 to 18 months on new oak
Almost black in colour. Enormous concentration in the nose, especially black fruit and torrefaction, mint and cocoa. Very powerful and concentrated in the onset. Wine with an impressive structure that needs time. Strong and yet smooth, ripe tannins. Lovely acids. A fruit bomb with an explosion of black fruit. Very long aftertaste. Majestic and impressive.

MAURO
MAURO
Vendimia Seleccionada
1996
Viñedos Propios
Vino de Mesa de Castilla y León
EMBOTELLADO POR BODEGAS MAURO, S.A.
TUDELA DE DUERO • VALLADOLID - ESPAÑA
14 % Alc/Vol.
Lote 01 R.E. 5776 - VA
750 Ml.

Hermanos Cuadrado García

Hermanos Cuadrado García
FINCA VILLACRECES
47350 Quintanilla de Onésimo
Tel.: 983 68 04 37
Fax: 983 23 90 00

Pedro Cuadrado

Owners: the Cuadrado García brothers

Manager: Pedro Cuadrado

Oenologists: Aubin Vergez, Peter Sisseck

Surface: 100 ha., including 50 ha. vineyards

Production: from 20,000 to 50,000 bottles

Type: red

The name of the domain refers to San Pedro de Villacreces who lived a secluded life here on his Ermita.

Finca Villacreces, a 'vin de garage' in Ribera del Duero

The 4 Cuadrado brothers were children in 'Finca Villacreces', the family estate on the riverbanks of the Duero. The estate has some 100 ha. in all, 50 of which are currently covered in vines. There used to be no more than 10 ha. vineyards in the past; the vines' yield would simply be sold. The estate is like an island, locked in an enclave with the village of Quintanilla de Onésimo, in Valbuena. Cuarado García's closest neighbour is Vega Sicilia, Valbuerta de Duero's leading bodega.

The story of the enclave goes back a long way. It is also quite incredible. The estate's owner in the 18th century would have been a gambler who was clever at throwing dice. He may not have been quite clever enough for, one day, he lost to an acquaintance of his in Quintanilla de Onésimo. The stakes had been… the estate. Not only did the winner get handed the certificate of ownership but the grounds added considerably to his own. The entire finca thus being transferred virtually overnight from Valbuena de Duero over to Quintanilla de Onésimo. At the time, it already felt like a small isle in the first village.

The history of Finca Villacreces goes back a lot further. Documents established by the Cistercian monks indicate there had been local vineyards as far back as the 13th century. In the last half of the 14th century, a small 'ermita' (chapel) stood on the spot where a saint, San Pedro di de Villacreces, had found refuge from the world. The saint gave his name to the entire estate. The Cuadrado brothers' grandparents had always lived on the Finca Villacreces. The boys parents moved to Valladolid. More vineyards were added to the estate over the years, the harvest was invariably bountiful and went for a good price later. But none of the brothers was really interested in running the estate: they all were far too busy with their own particular businesses.

Prompted by some revival in Spanish wine towards the mid-80's, Pedro Cuadrado finally thought of doing something with the place. He knew that the harvest had always been first

Pedro Cuadrado allows his grapes to ripen over an exceptionally long period.

In the middle of the domain, what used to be the stables have now been renovated into a small bodega.

class and some of the vines must have attained a lot of maturity. The estate's location, bordering onto Vega Sicilia as it was, also had something to be said for it. In 1985, Pedro Cuardo started planting Merlot, Cabernet Sauvignon and a little additional Tinto to Fino (Tempranillo), enough to cover the current 50 ha. surface.

Then Pedro started planning his own wine. The sort of project that never takes off right away... The state of the vineyards gradually improving, he selected a number of plots for that future wine of his. Luck was on his side: someone – a Dane, Peter Sisseck – took over the entire proceedings during a first millésime making, the millésime 1994. Sisseck had immigrated to Ribera del Douro with his family, without a word of Spanish and not knowing a soul. The village priest tried to coach the Sisseck's out of their isolation and introduced them to the Cuadrado's. It soon appeared Peter Sisseck was an inspired wine-maker and an excellent oenologist. An agreement was come to involving the vinification of the next harvest at the capable hands of Peter Sisseck. Production was restricted but the quality was superb: 9,000 bottles left the newly improvised bodega; the same few casks of concrete and inox

In this microclimate the Merlot ripens to an exceptional level.

The Duero which runs immediately behind the 100 ha. domain, forms the artery of the entire region.

used for millésime '94 were reused in the making of the Pingus, a wine to soar to untold heights later. Maybe the Pingus attained cult-status on account of its price (it is the most expensive wine in Spain!) but its quality was – and is – truly impressive. Peter Sisseck stayed on; he no longer is the only oenologist: in a same spirit, he addressed one of his friends, Aubin Vergez (an expert oenologist from Bordeaux) and introduced him to the estate. Vergez thereby also being appointed Finca Villacreces oenologist in 1995. 30,000 bottles millésime '98 have been produced so far. The quantity will never greatly increase, if to some anticipated 50,000 in the long term, owing to the vastness of the estate.

The harvest itself takes place a little late in the season. The Tempranillo or Tinto Fino is harvested towards the end of October. Cabernet Sauvignon and Merlot are harvested in November. The idea being to achieve maximum ripeness before picking the grapes. The Merlot most greatly gaining in quality here, to the point of it turning matchless throughout Ribera del Duero. The Finca Villacreces wines contain mostly Merlot (15%).

Merlot vineyards grow best on anything but ordinary soil. Since the estate's vineyards face the Duero and irrigation takes place towards the river, they are in the wake of alluvial erosion. The soil's substrata contain sand with a thick layer of pebbles on top. The soil the Merlot is on is completely covered in pebbles and grit. Both the Cabernet Sauvignon and the Merlot vines are closest to the river. Their grapes get fairly drenched at night, with the neighbourhood of the water. Their peel expands thereby, whilst the grapes themselves tend to shrink during the day, when the sun is out. The grapes thus being permanently 'active', one way or another. Yield moreover does not exceed the 3,000 kg/ha. very much. Pedro never applies weedkiller or pesticides, turning his wines into 'vinos ecologicos' this way.

At the start of the harvest, a selection is made from the various vineyards. Proportions in terms of quantity actually reaching the bodega are 10 to 1. On arrival, grapes are displayed again, on a selection table. After its maceration and fermentation periods, the wine is left on Allier oak. 50% of all barrels are new, their number increasing with the production.

The wine is bottled after 12 to 14 months. Pedro Cuadrado does not differentiate between traditional crianza and reserva denominations much: all wine reaches the market as crianza's. Depending on their basic structure, some wines stay 20 to 24 months on oak. Theoretically, these are the reserva's of remainder Ribera Del Duero bodega's. They are marketed under the label 'crianza especial'. Their quantity is usually fairly limited (2000 to 4000 bottles). New projects were set up in the meantime: a separate wine, the Pruno, was vinified from the grapes of a small vineyard covered in Tempranillo some 80 years old. No more than 200 bottles 'Pruno' were bottled in1998. Yet the futures is promising.

Range

2 red wines

Finca Villacreces crianza
75% Tinto fino, 15% Merlot, 10% Cabernet Sauvignon
12 months on French oak, including 50% new
Dark red in colour. A very intricate nose of black fruit, blackcurrant, coffee, chocolate liquorice, eucalyptus, mint and minerals. Fairly potent palate but well balanced and full with a huge dose of black fruit. A wine with a very young feel. Ripe tannins and well balanced acids. Long aftertaste.

Finca Villacreces Crianza Especial

75% Tinto fino, 15% Merlot, 10% Cabernet Sauvignon
24 months on French oak, including 50% new
Very dark gown, lovely oily belt. Also an intricate nose of black fruit, blackcurrant, coffee, chocolate, liquorice, eucalyptus, mint, minerals and a little toasted bread with whiffs of vanilla. Assertive start-off, massses of fruit. Takes quite a little time to find its balance: must be laid to rest a little longer. Its tannins are ripe. Pleasant and lithe acids. Extensive finale.

Export

80% of all production, mainly to the USA, Germany, Switzerland and Japan.

FINCA
VILLACRECES
RIBERA DEL DUERO
DENOMINACION DE ORIGEN
ELABORADO Y EMBOTELLADO
EN LA PROPIEDAD POR
HNOS. CUADRADO-GARCIA, C.B.
QUINTANILLA DE O. VALLADOLID (ESPAÑA)
75 cl e
13% Vol.
CRIANZA 1996
63 mm

Vega Sicilia

C. Nacional 122, km. 323
VEGA SICILIA
47359 Valbuena de Duero
Tel.: 983 68 01 47
Fax: 983 68 02 63

Pablo Alvarez

Owners: the Alvarez family

Manager delegate: Pablo Alvarez Mezquíriz

Technical manager: Xavier Ausás

Oenologists: Begoña Jovellar, Mercedes Ausás

Agronomist: Francisco Alonso

Surface: 1000 ha., including 250 ha. vineyards

Production: according to the year: 160,000 to 265,000 bottles + 200 to 350,000 bottles Alion

Type: red wine

The buildings were meticulously renovated and maintained by the Alvarez family.

The hard working 'número uno'

Vega Sicilia really is the wine estate with the richest history in Spain. In spite of its historic riches, Vega Sicilia has stayed one of the more modern amongst the Iberic peninsula's bodega's. Its current proprietor is defenitely no stranger to presentday successes: the Alvarez family, especially Pablo Alvarez, the bodega's big man at the top. Even with the Vega Sicilia's name and fame backing, he estimates this is hardly enough and one should not stand in the way of change. Change never takes place at the expense of tradition here. On the contrary: on this estate, the wine made now is the same as contained in the first bottles ever leaving Finca Vega Sicilia. But Alvarez is of his own time and he furthermore does not shun expense once a project needs to be put into practice. The Spanish world of wine has been constantly on the move over the past 10 years; the evolution is also closely followed on the spot. It was none too difficult for the estate to be winning candidate on the list to the top; but with the current revolutionary Spanish wine situation it might not always be equally easy to stay at the top, nevertheless.

Pablo Alvarez knows this only too well. Otherwise, he is fairly happy with the estate's position vis-à-vis current developments, if particularly with the Ribera del Duero appellation. In spite of this appellation's steady growth in recent years – particularly in Spain itself – it has not exceeded the start of square two in the field of new staging. Following the commercial success and mass plantations of the past few years, 80% of Ribera del Duero's current vineyards do not exceed the 10 years of age. A great deal of money has been invested also from outside the appellation. Spain is witnessing major economic growth and a boom in the field of wine production. This also means a lot of people with money and the love of wine like to invest in the sector.

Alvarez is nevertheless experienced enough to know all this is not quite as simple as it may first sound. His family bought the estate in 1982, only and because it happened to be Vega Sicilia. They otherwise would never have taken on the challenge. At the time too, it went for relatively small price.

The presence of a chapel illustates the – even religious – tradition Vega Sicilia relies on.

The remains of this aqueduct are to be found running through the domain.

A wine producing business can nevertheless not be run from an office somewhere in Madrid – new investors ought to mind the wine more and a little less the marketing and all kinds of trimmings surrounding it.

The economic boom is not all sweetness and light to Ribera del Duero. Lots of irregularities are in the picture at the moment, some bodega's produce good wine, others quite decent wine, but the majority makes poor quality wine. There is not enough experience and everything is to be ready at once. According to Alvarez, some 80% of all grapes were picked too soon in 1999, a fairly difficult but otherwise top year for the area. The quality of the region's wine may be expected to vary greatly as a result. The quantity however vastly increased in volume.

All may be better in time and the lesser gods may automatically be eliminated. It takes long to make good wine and it also is very expensive: patience is the better part of valour in this. Particularly when you consider that, during the time it took one Vega Sicilia Unico to ripen on barrel, some bodega's managed building a cellar, planted vineyards and already put 2 harvests on the market. Vega Sicilia is in an entirely different world. How did Vega Sicilia actually get to belong to that world?

It all started in 1848, when Don Toribio Lecanda – a Basque citizen – helped the Marqués de Valbuena overcome his financial troubles on buying the 2000 ha. estate off him. When Don Eloy Lecanda inherited the estate from his father, on July 22nd 1859 he decided to do something with it. In 1864 he went to Bordeaux and bought some 18,000 vines there: Cabernet Sauvignon, Carmenère, Malbec, Merlot and Pinot Noir. As he planted these in his Finca Vega Sicilia, many looked up in astonishment. The estate had mainly lived from cattle-rearing up to now, its orchards and making and selling ceramics.

When the Lecanda's also sailed into deep waters financially, new moneylenders appeared on the scene: the Herrero's. 15 years later, Antonio Herrero Velázquez had acquired the estate. In 1905, its management was entrusted one Txomin Garramiola. This Basque citizen had first worked for the Rioja bodega Cosme Palacio. Because there had been problems with clients in Bilbao following the phylloxera and the necessary supplies of wine could no longer be certified (Bilbao at the time being the commercial pivot in the field of wine, – particularly from Rioja) Antonio's sons suggested letting the bodega to Herrero – who had been responsible for the estate since 1901 – for a 10 year period. The Palacio took on Txomin and made him into their 'confidant'. It was he who would make the wine. The desired style would be determined by the wine the Cosme Palacio's clients were used to, or the Rioja's: extensive ripening on wood and bottling as the orders came in, no sooner. The estate then used to be called the 'Bodegas de Lecanda'.

When in 1915 the lease ran out and the estate was re-named 'Hijos de Antonio Herrero' the 3 brothers managed to convince Txomin to stay on. It was a mark of prestige to continue making wine. From that day Txomin could also produce his own wine but it would not be used in the way of a substitute in the case of a Rioja Cosme Palacio shortage.

The Herrero's moved in the very closed circles of the Spanish aristocracy and the big industrials of the day. The bodega was a losing activity but remainder Finca income was expected to fill the gap. It was never their intention to make a Vega Sicilia for commercialization. The wine was not for sale and was solely intended for Herrero prestige. The wine went to friends and could not be bought with money. If someone insisted he or she wanted a bottle anyway and he or she was no friend of the family, the Herrero's would charge a price out of all proportion by any standards of the day. This is how the myth of Spain's most expensive wine was born.

The 20's were the years of success throughout Europe. In 1933 Txomin died; the estate was sold to the seed producers Prodes in 1952. But the enthusiasm had left with the Herrero brothers until Jesús Anadón, who managed the estate until its owners sold it again.

It was bought by the Alvarez. And this was the best thing that could have happened to Vega Sicilia. They had acquired Finca Vega Sicilia in the way of an investment – the family business 'Eulen' is in the industrial maintenance and security sectors, and one of Spain's main company holdings. The Alvarez realised the thread must be picked up in the field of evolution; they never stopped investing in the estate. Vega Sicilia can also pride itself on the best equipment in the whole of Spain's bodega's.

As previously mentioned: the estate stays strong on tradition. Vega Sicilia still avails of a number of toneleria's where barrels are made or repaired. Barrels play an important role as a rule: the Vega Sicilia Unico stays some 7 years on wood, a totally unique concept anywhere in Europe. The choice is more than an exclusivity: it is a necessity. The wine really needs that long. Wines are no less than 10 years old when they are put on the market. The last production to reach it was the Unico 1990, a wine in its very prime according to the standards of the house.

Besides the estate's banner-carrier, the Vega Sicilia Unico, the Valbuena 5° año too was put on the market. Both wines must come from vines no less than 15 years old and optimal ripeness must have been achieved. Every vineyard is closely monitored during ripening; a decision will also be made then as to which grapes go to the Valbuena and which to the Unico. The expert knows from experience that, in practice, only the oldest vines' grapes are for Unico. Both the alcoholic and the malolactic fermentation happen in barrels of wood. Then the wine is put in different casks year after year, with different qualities each time. After bottling, the wine continues to ripen in the bottle as long as it will be considered necessary.

Many of the oak vats used by Vega Sicilia were made on site.

Another unique estate wine is the Vega Sicilia Unico Reserva Especial. It is created as it were by 150 years history. There did not used to be that many bodega's in Vega Sicilia's early days, that bottled their own wine. According to the rules of tradition, these bodega's solely bottled the best – the 'Vinos del Bodeguero' – blends of all the bodeguero's (or the bodega's owners) considered to be their best wines. The tradition lasted for dozens of years in Vega Sicilia. The wine too was a blend of years, inherent qualities, experience and feeling: a wine that is unique in the world.

For years – from 1968 to 1998 – the estate's oenologist had been Mariano García. He approved of the modernisation of the estate and made the wine into what it is now. Mariano retired onto his own estate in 1998, the Mauro . The technical leadership of Vega Sicilia was entrusted Xavier Ausás, a young oenologist with an ability of producing constant quality. His right hand, pretty Mercedes Ausás – his sister – is an equally clever oenologist.

The Alvarez' avail of a few more aces: for each Valbuena 5° año, before, there was a Valbuena 3er año. This wine did nevertheless not live up to requirements and a new project was set afoot. In 1986 a decision was come to the create a new bodega in Ribera del Duero, completely independent of Vega Sicilia and located in a different place. Some 25 ha. were acquired in 1987 and 18 ha. of these were covered in Tempranillo in 1988. A new bodega was bought in 1992, more towards Peñafiel in Padilla de Duero. Existing stocks were sold in the way of 31,900 bottles Alión 1991, still produced by the Vega Sicilia installations and heading for the market in 1995.

Since then the new creation kept on doing well. Pablo Alvarez insists Alion and Vega Sicilia have no connection, a more modern philosophy being involved. Between 1989 and the year 2000 some 125 ha. vineyards were planted on Finca Vega Sicilia soil. The Alion thus being in for perpetual improvement since only vines over the 9 years old can be used

for it. The wine is more attractive to the consumer who probably figures it better than a Vega Sicilia Unico. Some 350,000 Alion bottles will be produced in the future – the 1996 harvest having been the more exuberant up to now with some 305,588 bottles and 4,000 magnums.

Another project the Alvarez' strongly invested in was the DO Toro. From 1997 onwards, various pieces of land covered in old vines had been acquired. There had been some 14 ha. at first; now there are some 52 ha., – besides the 25 ha. with new plantations. In 1997, 1998 and 1999 a number of experiments in vinification were resorted to involving the various Toro plots. The grapes always were of the best possible quality but still needed 'training into shape' by the house. A first harvest is planned for 2001; it will be put on the market in 2005. It may well be worth closely following developments in the field…

Not only in Spain did the Alvarez manage investing: they also went looking abroad. Hungary e.g., where they tackled the Tokaj market. Oremus' was acquired and totally renovated. Liquid gold is produced here in the way of sweet Tokaj Aszú. But there is a virtual world of difference with the Ribera del Duero.

Inside the bodega the atmosphere is one of perfection and workmanship. Here we see the large oak vats.

Pablo Alvarez does not intend to stop thinking out projects. New ideas are in the offing. There undoubtedly will be new appellations following the Toro; and to them will be applied the Vega Sicilia philosophy of quality. This convinces us Spain is but at the dawn of yet another wine-revolution.

Range

3 red wines

Valbuena 5° año
80% Tempranillo, 15% Cabernet Sauvignon, Malbec, Merlot
36 months on oak, including 80% American and 20% French
Dark red in colour. Pleasant nose with hints of spice and a nice touch of wood into the background. Palate has powerful start-off with masses of fruit and acids clearly present. Body needs settling and developing. May take some time. Tannins are flexible and ripe. Long aftertaste.

Vega Sicilia Unico
Is minimum 10 years old, maximum 20 on reaching the market – but for the odd exception.
80% Tempranillo, 15% Cabernet Sauvignon, Malbec, Merlot
On oak as long as necessary and no less than 7 years
Virtually ink-black in colour. Very lively nose with masses of black fruit, cocoa, leather, chocolate and coffee. Palate starts off lithe with a lot of midriff strength, well balanced body with lots of tannins and acids, but most of all a riot of black fruit, all perfectly balanced. Savoury in the mouth. Gives the impression of being both ready for consumption and having quite a little time ahead. Eternally young. Brilliant finale. Grand and youthful.

Vega Sicilia, Unico Reserva Especial
A blend of wines from a different year
Very dark-red with a pleasant evolution. Mysterious nose in which you try to detect a number of different millésimes. Elegant fruit, nicely integrated wood, leather, chocolate, coffee and balsamic herb overtones. Palate that is both lithe and strong. All the better facets of the various millésimes together in one same wine. Superbly balanced – fruit, tannins, acids. Vastly intricate. Very extensive finale that keeps vibrating. Mysterious and majestic. Authentic and quite unique.

Export:

35% of all production to 44 different countries.

VEGA-SICILIA
COSECHA 1990
"UNICO"
Ribera del Duero
Denominación de Origen
Medalla de Oro y Gran Diploma de Honor
Feria de Navidad de Madrid de 1927
Medalla de Oro y Gran Diploma de Honor
Exposición Hotelera de Barcelona de 1927
Gran Premio de Honor
Exposición Internacional de Barcelona 1929-30
75Cl.
13.5%Vol.
EMBOTELLADO EN LA PROPIEDAD
BODEGAS VEGA SICILIA, S. A.
VALBUENA DE DUERO (Valladolid) España
Esta cosecha ha sido escogida para ser embotellada
en 109.548 botellas bordelesas, 2.653 magnum y
doble magnum.
El número de esta botella es el № 20353
BODEGAS VEGA SICILIA, S. A.
El Presidente
LOTE N.º 041

Pazo de Señorans

Vilanoviña
Pazo de Señorans
36616 Meis
Tel.: 986 71 55 74
Fax: 986 71 55 69

Marisol Bueno en Javier Mareque

Owners: Marisol Bueno en Javier Mareque

Manager: Ramón Iglesias

Oenologist: Ana Quintela

Surface: 10 ha. in ownership and 8.5 ha. under supervision

Production: varying from 150,000 to 190,000 bottles

Type: white

Beautifully situated, the Pazo with a small chapel in the middle

The Albariño of Madam President

Rias Baixas is a newcomer onto the Spanish DO scene. This appellation nevertheless soon acquired quite a reputation for quality. It may well be the result of good leadership also: the DO's lady-president, Marisol Bueno, per chance also the owner of Pazo de Señorans, and the determination and spirit she has shown up to now, accounting for it. Her being at the head of an own estate is not really 'by chance' anyway; for, there too, surfaces this concern with standards for own products.

There is a long wine-making tradition in Galicia, particularly in inland Galicia and the more hilly Ribiero country. Rias Baixas nevertheless staying the more famous appellation by far in this green region of Spain. The DO always insisted on quality from the moment it was set up. It was not necessarily the easiest of terms… But it had been Marisol Bueno's rule, and one she would abide by from the moment she was appointed DO president in 1988. In fact, the DO itself was only created in 1988. It was to be called 'Albariño' at first, after the region's most popular grape. The E.U. ruled against however. So, it was eventually re-named 'Rias Baixas'.

At the time Marisol did not own any wine herself. She had no experience or past connections with the wine sector before taking on the Pazo de Señorans challenge. She arrived from the Basque country in Galicia upon marrying Javier Mareque; he nevertheless had some background in oenology. The couple lived in the historic centre of Pontevedra but was more attracted to life in the country. In 1979 they decided to buy Pazo de Señorans, a truly wonderful estate, with a fabulous historic past. It lay at the heart of Val do Salnes, in the village of Meis. Pazo de Señorans is a brilliant example of rural historic architecture: there are the 'pazo' or mansio itself, a small bodega, a typical local 'horreo' or grain-storage barn and even a small chapel, in blocks of chopped granite every one of them. All these constructions also dating back to the 14th century; they say that, at the time, the estate stretched much further than the 10 ha. it is on now.

The front of the chapel has been meticulously renovated.

Throughout the domain are granite remains of the first building that dates back to the 14th century.

The Alberiño grows in pergolas so as to protect the grapes from the rain.

There is very little precise documentation on Pazo de Señorans' past history; it seems Manuel II, the last king of Portugal stayed at the Pazo towards the start of 20th century; from there, he tried to conduct actions against Franco's dictatorship (Meis is quite close to the border with Portugal). Manuel II was successful in his actions at first and stayed king from 1908 to 1910. But he was only 20 and he turned out powerless in the face of the revolution of October 4th 1910. He was forced to flee to London and died there in 1932.

The last king of Portugal had good taste! Pazo de Señorans is undoutedly one of the most beautiful places in Galicia (maybe even in the whole of Spain). Fortunately, this example of architectural patrimony was rescued when Javier and Marisol decided to buy it in 1979. First, they began restoring the terraces that had been laid on in the grounds. At the time, kiwi's were growing there; the kiwi's had to go and make place for the Albariño vines.

The Albariño is traditional of Galicia and responsible for the prosperity of the area that practically depends on it. Involved is a grape that, if properly vinified, is likely to give the best possible results. Research revealed its origins to probably lay in Germany, through Riesling clone selection brought over by German monks to the North-West of Spain. The Albariño vine also grows in Portugal. Whilst warranting the quality of a true Spanish white wine, the standards of the 'Alvarinho' in the 'Vinho verde' are questionable, for too often destined to mass production and on the cheap. The grape is small with a high sugar

The Alberiño grows on the slopes on a substratum of granite in an exceptional microclimate.

The 'Horreo' or granary, that is still to be seen in its original form all over Galicia.

content. It has the particularity of bringing out the every feature of the soil it grows in. All these things owing to the goodly disposition of the Riesling grape itself.

They also are the reasons why Marisol is a strong believer in the Albariño. The bodega only uses that specific type of grape and it is the basis of the two wines produced on the estate now. Marisol even refuses the coupages applied throughout another 'sub-zone' in Rias Baixas, O Rosal, South of Val do Salnes and near the border with Portugal. A mere 70% Albariño is used there, topped with Treixadura and Loureira. The German Riesling's being Marisol's favourite wines, a number of trips to Riesling country prompted her to start experimenting with botrytis, without definite results so far. But she does not go into a gloom for that much: it took her 11 years (until 1991) to bring a first wine out. She did manage it however.

In her capacity of the DO's chairman Marisol wanted to most of all set an example: her wine would be the shining proof of the many possibilities the Albariño had to offer, something that was not altogether as easy as it appeared. But Marisol set her target and eventually reached it. Her husband, Janvier, was far too busy with his famous surgery practice in Pontevedra to see to wine-making much. So she began to be re-equip the house's bodega herself in 1989; tiny, made-to-measure inox casks, fitting well into the restricted spaces of the initial bodega, started to be brought in.

A first millésime, the Pazo de Señorans 1990 then reached the market in a mere 7,000 bottles. Madam Presidente had kept her promise: the wine was (and today, more than ever, is!) a grand example of what can be achieved, and one for the entire DO to see.

In 1991 she had the support of a clever oenologist, Ana Quintela (another woman!); Ana had a Master in Oenology. She was expected to improve standards even more for the quality of the house's top-wine, to first be vinified in 1995: the Pazo de Señorans Selección de Añada. The wine had everything from beginning to end. Its ripening, to start off with: a 'vendange tardive' is involved here. Ana thereby wanting to encourage her Albariño's fully ripening. The density of the wine is quite exceptional for a white wine. Selection and density bordering onto the never-before witnessed. No other Albariño is quite as rich and full of minerals: there is perfect harmony of soil and fruit.

Then there is the finish of the wine, Marisol and Ana going well against all present-day trends in the field of wood as applied to wine. Marisol is determined: 'I do not have the slightest intention of making wines tasting of wood; I want my wines to stay the expres-

sion of my own terroir to the last, and the expression of the Albariño, a grape too subtle in itself and one that would be crushed beyond recognition using new oak…' Tasting sessions of trendy Albariño's ripened on wood proved her to be right: these wood-like wines often have an akward and bombastic temperament, without the slightest hint of finesse. They also age badly.

Marisol and Ana thereby also going against more trends of the day in Rias Baixas: the trend to make wines to be consumed within the year, expensive easy-drinkers to be consumed as quickly as possible. The Selección de Añada gets its ripening in inox for 2 to 3 years, depending on the oenologist's decision. Only then is it bottled. The wine still retaining all of its fraîcheur at the time of bottling, yet also ready revealing its capacity to age well. Rias Diaz' soil contents in granite find their full expression in these wines, with traces of minerals everywhere. The future will certainly tell if the wine manages to age well and whether it eventually develops more terroir the way only a Riesling can.

The small cuverie has now been extended and transferred from the old countryhouse to a bodega hewn into the rock.

Another novelty is the 'Orujo', an Albariño marc, reaching up to actual wine level already. Its production is quite restricted today. The bodega in the meantime expanding qua equipment and available land. The total vineyard surface currently representing 18.5 ha. A new hall is being dug out of the rock beneath the surface to manage working even more efficiently in an underground space later.

You will never hear Ana or Marisol boast about it (discretion staying the better part of valor to them!), but there has been many a testimony so far – both in Spain and abroad – as to the excellence of the wine that is being produced on the estate. This, people say, is the best white wine in Spain…

Range

2 white wines

Pazo de Señorans
Albariño 100%
A lovely golden gown. Intensely florid nose with hints of minerals. Amidst the flowery overtones are found nice touches of exotic fruit, peaches, grapefruit, tangerines and honey. Very full palate. The acids are perfectly well balanced. A great deal of fraîcheur, Fruitiness and exuberance. But also intricate and well proportioned. A brilliant accompaniment to shellfish and seafood.

Pazo de Señorans, Selección de Añada
100% Albariño
A beautiful bright yellow colour. Intricate nose of fruit and minerals: a terroir-nose, almost sweet, in quite an unobtrusive way. Very rich palate with much fruit and depth. Attractive acids and a very lengthy aftertaste. Terrific class. White topper.

Export

22% of all production, mainly to the USA and Britain.

RIAS BAIXAS
Denominación de Origen
PAZO DE SEÑORANS
Albariño
1999
RIAS BAIXAS
12% vol. 75cl.
Product of Spain

Viña Mein

Mein- San Clodio
Viña Mein
32429 Leiro
Tel.: 988 48 84 00
Fax: 988 48 87 32
E-mail: vinamein@worldaline.es

Javier Alen

Owner: Javier Alen

Oenologist: Emilio Vidal

Agronomist: Ricardo Vazquez

Area: 12 ha.

Production: varying annually between 25,000 and 93,000 bottles

Type: 97% white
3% red

The area around Viña Mein is the origin of all Ribeiro's vines.

The lawyer becomes a wine farmer

The appellation of Ribeiro is the oldest appellation of Galicia. This green province that is situated in the far northwest of Spain has a long history of wine growing. The wines of Ribeiro were well-known throughout Spain as far back as the 12th century, and they were also the first to be exported abroad. At that time the best-known wines were mainly white wines. The Treixadura grape was (and still is) mainly responsible for this. This grape was known as the 'gran dama blanca' – the great white lady – also referred to as the queen of the white grape, and was recorded as being the most complex and the most exuberant of all. This grape is unique in Spain and is not found anywhere else. Its origin is not clear and although the grape used to have a good name, it has enjoyed very little interest during this century. We have had to wait for Javier Alen to bring it into the limelight once more.

The Treixadura grape was without doubt Javier's very first solid food that he ate as a baby. He has carried the memory of it with him all his life. When he was six he moved to Madrid with his parents, but memories of the region where he was born came to life during the summer months when the family would move to their ancestral home in Leiro for three months. Javier spent the rest of his youth in Madrid. He became a lawyer and worked as a partner for more than 15 years for the well-known American office of Baker & Mc Kenzie in Madrid. Nevertheless, his busy life filled him with memories of his youth and far-off Galicia. It was for this reason that Javier gave up his lawyer's office and started a bookshop in Madrid that was specialised in travel literature from all over the world. He then decided to return to his beloved Leiro and become a wine farmer there.

The village of Leiro is situated in the province of Orense which lies in the river valleys of the Amoya, the Avia and the Mino. The whole appellation area is located in this province and extends over a wine area of 3000 ha. The vineyards are usually situated in the hills that slope down to one of the three rivers. This geographical feature is also referred to in the name of the appellation: 'Ribeiro' is Gellego for 'riverbank'. The surface is therefore mostly alluvial sand containing lots of fine granite – 'sabrego' in Gallego – in view of the fact that the substratum is this area consists wholly of granite.

The whole domain exudes an atmosphere of peace and quiet: everything is in harmony with nature.

Without doubt, this is one of the most charmingly romantic wine domains in Spain.

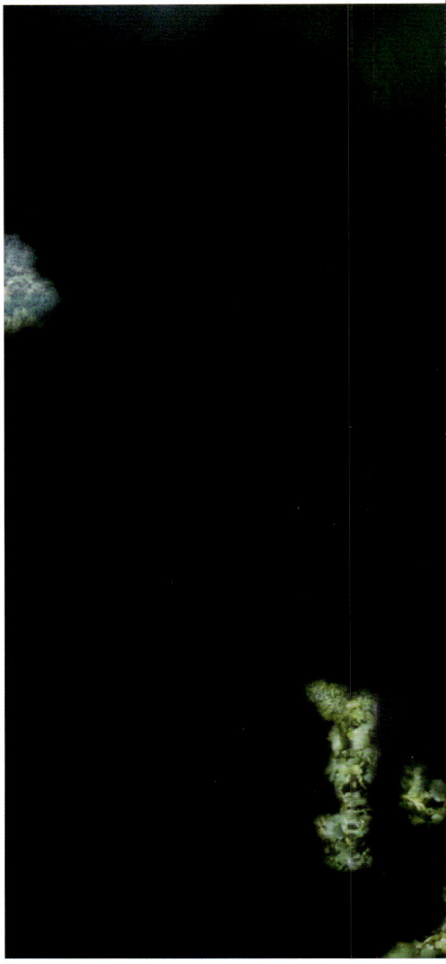

The area surrounding the domain of Vina Mein has a rich history. Immediately in front of this small domain lies the now fully renovated San Clodio monastery. This monastery was founded in the 11th century by Benedictine monks. As in other regions in Spain, these monks brought with them holy water as well as wine and vineyards. The red vines that were imported have a very clear origin. Indeed, in the Mencía grape we find characteristics that are very similar to those of the Cabernet Franc: a fair amount of rain with an average temperature that is not too high, although it can get very hot here in the summer. The area around Vina Mein is where all the vines in Ribeiro originally come from. It was here that the first vines were planted by the Benedictine monks. The wine was distributed by pilgrims travelling to Santiago de Compostela.

Together with a few friends, Javier Alen bought the Vina Mein domain in 1987. It lay right in front of Alen's ancestral home which is situated a little higher, and overlooks the domain. The house had already been an important 'finca agricola' in the 17th century, and is supported by a huge block of granite against which it is quite literally built. The domain had always been one of the most important rural domains in the region, as the rest consisted mainly of country cottages surrounded by a bit of land. Until the early thirties there had

been a small village around the domain consisting of about 12 houses each with their own bit of land. Indeed, the land in Galicia has been very fragmented since time immemorial. During the 20th century the domain was owned by the Fabrega family, an important pharmaceutical family from Orense. Wine was made on the domain until the beginning of the seventies, after which it was abandoned and consequently became dilapidated. When Javier bought the domain it needed a lot of work: unfortunately nothing could be done to save the vines as these had been almost completely neglected for 20 years. However, hard work and a certain amount of financial investment turned the house into a beautiful whole. The house was completely renovated: former rooms were turned into gues-rooms furnished in the typically rural style of Galicia. A small modern bodega was built in addition to this. The architect successfully and very elegantly managed to integrate the modern elements with the rural surroundings of the domain, forming a whole that is perfectly lovely. Cuves inox were installed in the bodega as well all the modern machinery that is needed to produce a high quality white wine.
Because the vines could not be recovered after having grown wild for so many years, he started planting anew; the grape was Treixadura, a grape which Javier believed in and wanted to

[redacted]

[redacted]

The monastery of San Clodio lies barely 500 m from the domain. From here the monks distributed the Treixadura vine.

The monastery was recently fully renovated to become a 'Parador'.

help it recover its earlier fame. Loureira, Godello, Torrontès, Albarino, Albilla and Lado were also used, but to a lesser extent. Javier firmly believed in blending his Treixadura with a minor amount of other types of grapes. He managed to partly recover the red vines: indeed, still growing on the domain is a certain amount of Caino Longo which is a species of grape that has now become rare in the rest of Galicia. Javier's red wine is the only wine to have this type of grape in the assemblage.

In 1994 with the aid of Emilio Vidal – a well-known oenologist in Ribeiro – he managed to vinify his first white wine, 'Casal del Mein', which did not pass unnoticed in Spain. The first red wine was vinified in 1996, the Tinto Clásico: a blend of Mencía and Caino Longo. Finally he made an orujo of Treixadura, which is a very high quality distillation with a high level of complexity.

The white wines proved to have an enormous fraîcheur and concentration, but were only made in limited quantities during the first vintages. During the first 5 vintages production consistently amounted to between 15 to 20 thousand bottles. It was only in 1999 that Javier achieved the agreed number of 9,000 bottles. By now the wine had acquired a name abroad, but it was mainly in Spain that it became an established name and regarded as the quality wine of Ribeiro. It was also this wine that ensured that the Treixadura once more acquired a special place on the wine list. Moreover, this wine goes very well together with the typical Galician specialities of crustaceans and shellfish. The concentration of fruit and minerals in the terroir form an excellent combination.

Javier now had even more plans for the future: in 2000 a 100% Treixadura was made for the first time, and one that was even more highly concentrated with a fermentation in its own large 3000 litre vat. With this he returned to tradition. Indeed, in the past vinification in Galicia was only done in large wooden vats. The result is a modern wine that is linked to the age-old Galician tradition. Through Javier Alen Ribeiro can once more be proud of its ancient wine legacy. Because of him the Treixadura has been restored to its former glory.

The house and bodega are surrounded by the queen of the Ribeiro: the Treixadura.

Range

1 white wine

Viña Mein, Casal de Mein
70% Treixadura, 15% Godello, 8% Loureira, 3% Torrontès, 2% Albariño, 2% Albilla and Lado
Clear, pale yellow in colour, A complex nose with citrus, plenty of minerals (terroir!), grapefruit and zest. In addition to this, the typical character of the Treixadura gives it a fine spicy flavour. In the mouth an onset with plenty of fraîcheur. Concentration and minerals in the midriff. Spicy aftertaste with a lovely and subtle ending.

1 red wine

Viña Mein Tinto Clásico
50% Mencía, 50% Caiño longo
maturing on French oak
Clear red colour. Lovely, original nose, green paprika, wood undertone, red fruit, pepper, a hint of leather and minerals. A lot of fraîcheur in the mouth and beautifully structured with the presence of tannins and fruit. Slightly drier towards the finale, with a slight bitterness that is typical of the terroir. Wine for connoisseurs.

Export

15% of the production, mainly Belgium, Germany and the USA.

RIBEIRO
VIÑA
MEIN
S.L.
Casal de Mein
EMBOTELLADO EN LA PROPIEDAD
75 cl.
Nº R.E. OR-7470
12%
De la cosecha de 1999 se han elaborado
90.000 botellas con la noble cepa
Treixadura en un 70% y la Godello
en un 15%, siendo el resto una mezcla
de las otras variedades gallegas.

Toro Albalá

Ctra. General de Málaga 1
TORO ALBALÁ
14920 Aguilar de la Frontera
Tel.: 957 66 00 46
Fax: 957 66 14 94
E-mail: sorgato@talbala.com

Antonio Sánchez

Owner: Antonio Sánchez Romero

Daily guided tour: Francisco Muñoz Herrador

Oenologist: Antonio Sánchez Romero

Agronomist: Antonio Sánchez Romero

Surface: 35 ha.

Production: 280,000 bottles

Type: fino, amontillado, Pedro Ximenez

Antonio Sanchez' laboratory is never idle. There is always something new going on.

Antonio Sánchez, the Father of sweet wine

Does the wine grow like its maker or the maker like its wine? Whatever the outcome: both Antonio Sanchez and his wine, the Toro Albalá, are truly phenomenon in Spain. The bodega is a museum cum wine cellar cum curiosa cum rare wine collection medley. It is completely different from any other bodega's also within own region.

The said region itself is exceptional. Its DO Montilla-Moriles is in the midst of Córdoba, more specifically: just South of the town of the same name. Cordoba is extraordinarily beautiful. There are many indications and names, throughout the villages and towns, reminding of this district's golden age under Moorish rule. Everyone, Arabs and Jews included, lived in harmony and the entire area flourished. Many buildings still bear witness to this: think of the magnificent 'Mezquita' in Córdoba, e.g. So do books and documents – e.g. the Ibn Haqil.

The DO is near Montilla and Moriles, as its name will indicate. Montilla is a decent size town, Morilles more of a village. Toro Albalá is found in Aguilar de la Frontera, half way on the border separating the two. Montillo-Morilles wine is often compared to sherry. Not without a cause: until 1933 Montilla was part of the sherry district. It even had a better reputation than Jerez itself, at the time. The quality of the grape, the unique Pedro Ximenez being at the root of the former connoisseurs' choice. The grape would have been named after a soldier from the Flemish legion of the Spanish king who fought against the Moor's, one Peter Symens. The soldier was supposed to have brought to vine species to Cordoba, where his (then the vine's) name was difficult to pronounce and turned into Pedro Ximenez. Whether entirely true or not, it sounds plausible enough...

The Pedro Ximenez grows mainly here and is not readily found elsewhere in the world. If so, it will be in very small quantities. In Montillo virtually all grapes are Pedro Ximenez. The grape is unpopular elsewhere as it is slightly 'difficult' to manage. It has a very delicate

peel and is hyper-sensitive to oxidation thereby. The grape thus better lending itself to the making of 'oxide' wines like sherry and sweet wine types.

It may not surprise you the sherry named 'amontillado' originated in Montilla. The explanation is the following: the fino's that were produced in the area in the past were often exported to Jerez, because the Montilla fino had a better reputation. But the journey was not without its risks: it was long, the roads were bad and the heat was simply too much to bear at times. 'Fino' arriving in Jerez had also been the victim of these circumstances. It had undergone chemistry that turned it slightly brown. The browner the fino, the more likely it was to be called 'a montilladed wine'. This is how the 'amontillado' 's final denomination came about.

An important difference with actual sherry remaining the Montilla-Moriles wines are not built up. The grapes attain a 14° to 16° sugar content. Mostly involved, in this case, are the dry fino's, amontillado's and oloroso's, later undergoing a solera- and criadera process, like a sherry. The ripening takes 2 years minimum. Toro Albalá 's youngest fino is a 5 year old, the 'fino and rama'. The more mature 'fino del lagar' mostly ripens over a good many years and is a little greener in its colour. This would be specifically due to the grape, selected in Moriles by Toro Albalá for its 'Fino del lagar'.

Trumps for the area (including and mostly Bodegas Toro Albalá) are its sweet wines. One can honestly say Toro Albalá's ripening cellars are hidden treasures chambers, full of their sweet wines, slowly ripening over dozens of years. They are unique in the world.
Toro Albalá 's rich history is no stranger to this; nor is Antonio Sánchez, a sworn perfectionist, who knows what each and everyone of the bota's (the traditional ripening barrels) contains, where it is to be found, what the wine used to be like and what its evolution is likely to be.

The bodega's story goes back quite a bit, to the year 1844. In 1922 the house moved into the premises of a discarded electric-power plant, still home to the present-day bodega. An

amusing reminder of the past is the name 'Joven Eléctrico' given to young wine. It is also a kind of village joke and used as another word for 'drunk' (the word having turned into 'electrocutado' instead of 'borracho'). Rather obviously with Toro Albalá wine in mind!

The move to the electricity plant had been organised by the current owner, Antonio Sánchez's uncle, J.M. Toro Albalá. The bodega was continually modernized from then on and a considerable number of 'botas' were constructed, to each be stocked with sweet wine and amontillado 'crème de la crème'! Like the Convento 1939, a dark and sweet Pedro Ximenez with an endless aftertaste and very intricate in its structure. Or the same sweet Pedro Ximenez in its 1945 version, the Marqués de Poley. Or the Pedro Ximenez 1960. Each and everyone of them a preciosity, every bit as unusual as they are rare.

These wines are not the only Antonio Sánchez' collector items: there are those 'statements of history' and anything and everything you can possibly imagine in the field of wine-making throughout the ages: all meticulously gathered into a museum by Antonio himself. Then, there are those Roman coins, the axes dating back to the stone age, all that may have the slightest historic value and found in the DO Montilla-Moriles vineyards or even without... It has been card-indexed, classified, given a name...You will even find a the skeleton of a Roman slave there – and virtually intact! – complete with sinister iron chains dangling from its neck and one of its feet.

This collector's passion is not without its occasional problems, as Antonio Sorgato, the commercial manager for export explains: if a million pesetas worth in export has to go to a determined place and a Roman amphora has been dug up in the village nearby, the find being worth two million, Antonio Sanchez' choice will soon be made: the amphora shall be his!

Antonio Sanchez is always busy. With his wine, the history of wine, oenology in general; far less with the actual sale of his wine, something not altogether keeping him awake at night. The commercial side of things simply is not for him. But what a great and captivat-

pp. 198-199 The skeleton of a Roman slave with chained neck and feet was found in the vineyard.

Any moment a divine amontillado from 1950 will flow into the small glass…

It is compulsory for all celebrities who visit the bodega to autograph their own vat.

Some of the vats in this treasury have been lying waiting for dozens of years. However, nobody here is in a hurry.

ing personality he is! Welcoming and sociable, with a talent for narrating, sense of humor pigmenting all his conversations. He once came upon the idea of organizing a mass tasting event in Aguilar de la Frontera's main market square. This 'degustation' for 2000 people entered Antonio in the Guinness Book of Records. Many a big name from home and abroad had been invited to the tasting. The 'Cata popular' being over, everyone was asked back to the cellars of Toro Albalá, the place where Antonio feels at home most.The Pedro Ximenez and the amontillado flowing from the best barrels of the century all night. The climax was the moment of the ' grabbing' of the 'jamón de pata negra' from the ridge of the ripening-cellar: only those who had just over the few recommended glasses managed the leap. With a further amantillado encouragment as a prize and Antonio's broad grin!

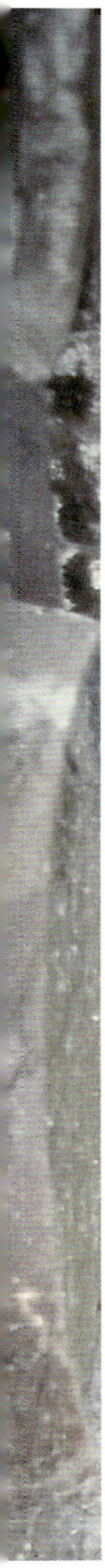

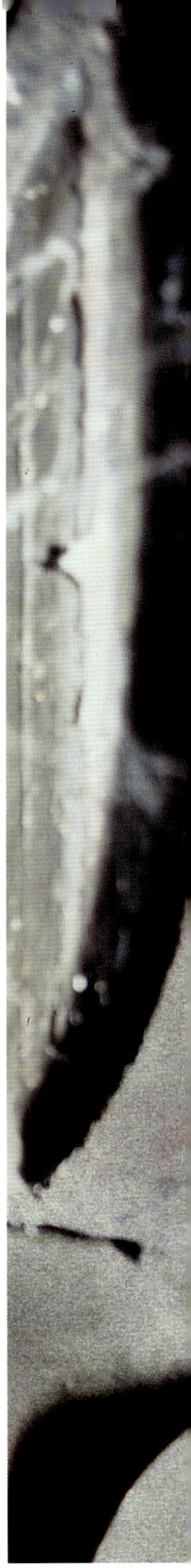

Toro Albalá can take a little fun every now and then and goes on regardless: it too chose the path of avant-garde and modernizing combined with tradition; it stayed with it as yet. A champion of the sweet Pedro Ximenez and the only bodega to manufacture the 'Don P.X.' so far a sweet Pedro Ximenez wine that does not get layered on wood but on inox casks. Results are amazing: a wine that is both pure and dense. The bodega has the Pedro Ximenez (and the way this wine is made) totally under control. The grapes are picked rather late in the season and left to dry on mats in the sun, the 'pasera'. This mostly takes place on a large scale and after the harvest but it is also a process that must be carefully monitored. Antonio supervises some 95% of the area's pasera's. Many appeal to him for knowledge and experience.

Antonio is also a pioneer of the joven afrutado, a white wine made with unripe grapes in order to prevent oxidation. Then fruity summery wines can be come to, without criadera. The labels are carefully chosen: handwritten labels of wood go onto the more valuable bottles. These are small masterpieces at the rate of 1 to 2 labels per day!

The word 'stale' is definitely out in Toro Albalà: things must keep evolving. Another bodega was recently acquired in Lucena e.g.; 2200 botas were in it. Even more recently a vineyard and a wine cellar in Moriles 'el Melgar'; the vineyard had some 37 ha. in all; 7 ha. will be destined to ecologic wine production. Antonio Sánchez and his assistants – his son-in-

De pasera: the overripe grapes are spread out on mats to dry under the scorching Cordovan sun.

law, Paco Muñoz and commercial export manager, Antonio Sorgato have many plans for the future, hoping to counteract the unfortunate general downward trend of the Montilla-Moriles wines for the moment. The seductive, intricate and immensely sensual quality-wines produced on the Toro Albalà estate helping to bend the trend in their favour.

An exceptional bodega altogether, with outstanding wines made by an inimitable character in a very special area.

Range

Fino en rama
100% Pedro Ximenez
with a solera some 5 years old
Yellow in colour. A pristine nose with lots of little nuts and toast, the spiciness of a crianza, brininess. A fairly full palate, spicy overtones. Beautiful and equilibrated aftertaste.

Fino del lagar
100% Pedro Ximenez
with a solera over 5 years old
Yellow in colour with a green hue. The very intense nose of a crianza rather than a fino or a rama. Nuts, spices. Much fuller and stronger palate. Predominantly briny. Long aftertaste.

Joven Eléctrico
100% Pedro Ximenez
Light green in colour. A pleasant nose of exotic fruit, melon and touches of brininess. Very cool palate also slightly briny. Fruity. A perfect thirst quencher.

Don P.X.
100% Pedro Ximenez
Slightly tawny colour. An intense nose of figs, dates and raisins. Very sweet start-off, full and immensely dense. Almost syrupy with sufficient acids added. Very extensive end.

Don P.X. Gran Reserva 1972
100% Pedro Ximenez
A dark tawny, almost black. Sweet bouquet, raisins, fig-paste, caramel, scalding, cocoa and nice wood in the nose. A sweet palate to start-off with sufficient acidity, nicely dense, full, delightfully sweet ending. Very extensive aftertaste.

Amontillado, Viejisimo solera 1922
100% Pedro Ximenez
Tawny, briny bouquet, spicy with fried fruits: nuts and hazelnuts, cocoa, coffee. A fine biologic crianza with enough fruit. Solid palate, partial to spicy nuts. Long aftertaste.

Convento, P.X. 1939
100% Pedro Ximenez
Dark tawny, almost black in colour. Sweet bouquet, raisins, fig-paste, caramel, scalding, cocoa. Enormously intricate. Slightly more sophisticated than the young Pedro Ximenez, has more acids but also a full palate; pleasant sweetness. Rounded, with a kind of inherent fraîcheur. Very long aftertaste.

Marqués de Poley, P.X. 1945
100% Pedro Ximenez
Dark tawny, with a golden hue. Sweet bouquet, raisins, figs, dates, scalding, cocoa and pleasant wood in the nose. Gentle palate, very agreeable sweetness. Highly intricate, sweet and briny notes with intertwining acidity. Vastly dense. Very lengthy aftertaste.

Export

Mainly to Belgium, Denmark, France, Japan and the USA

Botella Nº 1010
Vino de alta calidad
de las Bodegas
protegido por la
Denominación de Origen
Serie 54 de botellas 1540
de 75 Cl. y Alc. 17 Vol.
Es un DON PX
de la cosecha 1961
seleccionado y garantizado
por Antonio Sánchez
Aguilar de la Frontera (Córdoba)
N.E. 6943 - Co.

Gutiérrez Colosía

Avda. Bajamar 40
Gutiérrez Colosía
11500 El Puerto de Santa María
Tel.: 956 85 28 52
Fax: 956 54 29 36
E-mail: gcolosia@teleline.es

Juan-Carlos Gutiérrez Colosía

Owner: María Loreto Colosía

Daily guided tour: Juan-Carlos Gutiérrez Colosía and Carmen Pou

Production: 4000 bottles (with naves de crianza and botas of some 2,000,000 l)

Type: fino, amontillado, palo cortado, oloroso, moscatel soleado, Pedro Ximenez

The 'naves de crianza' with their 'birth date': 1838

The best kept secret in sherryland

Bodegas Gutiérrez Colosía is one of the region's smaller sherry-bodega's. As an almacenista it survived the heavy crisis afflicting the sherry production in the course of the 70's and 80's. This survival capacity representing a reference in itself!
The bodega is run by Juan-Carlos Gutiérrez Colosía, his wife, Carmen Pou and Carmen Renedo. The team manages bottling one of the world's best sherries. The bodega had always functioned like an almacenista: wine ripening in its 'naves de crianza', kept well fed and sold on to the larger companies. These, in turn, put the wine on the market. The quality managed by this bodega stayed a closely kept secret with the larger sherry houses. But in 2000 – and fortunately for us – Gutierez Colosía chose to bottle their own wine. It was a success!

Even if the 'bottling affair' is quite recent, the history of the estate appears to be the opposite. It goes back to 1838. El Puerto de Santa María was a favourite point of departure for emigrants to Northern America. Gutiérrez Dosal – Juan-Carlos' grandfather – came down from Santander and settled in El Puerto; he started a business catering for the emigrants and the visiting ships. He began a workshop with fuel. Next to it, and as usually is the case, came a 'taberna', to better accommodate the clients. All this was happening in the Guadalete area that had the cheapest land at the time (with a lot of 'riff-raff' from the harbour). But José Gutiérrez knew that part of El Puerto like his pocket. The neighbourhood, 'Campo de Guia', had a number of bodega's in it. There also used to be a small chapel in Campo de Guia ('ermita'), dedicated to the 'Virgen de la Guia', the sailors' guardian saint; the Madonna was invoked as a guide ('guia') of ships and is represented holding a torch. Some remainders of the chapel still stand within the walls of the old bodega. The present-day bodega was set up in 1838 by 2 owners: García Gastón and De Castriciones. It further was owned by the Gutiérrez Colosía's, between 1910 and 1920.

Juan-Carlos, who runs it now, was virtually born amidst wine and wine bottles. As a child he played between the botas in the naves de crianza. At 14 – in 1960 – he already worked in

It is hard to imagine a better situation for a maturation cellar for sherry: right on the banks of a river mouth.

The naves de crianza seen from the opposite side of the Guadalete

the bodega; when his father died in 1966, he took over with his brother. Together they decided to keep the business going. At the time, they were active as 'criadores de vino' (literally: 'wine educators') or 'almacenistas' (keepers). Almacenistas are few and far between in El Puerto de Santa María today. The smaller almacenistas, like Gutiérrez Colosía who managed to survive the crisis, produce top-class wine right now, however. They also were lucky enough to avail of the best 'basis', the wine itself in other words.

Juan-Carlos remembers how things started going downhill for sherry towards the end of the 60's-early 70's. Firstly owing to increasing demand – with more and more plantations (vineyards even doubling in a matter of years). When demand started to stagnate and even dropped the larger bodega's had excess wine everywhere. They opted to sell it on the cheap rather than keep it. Prices increasingly fell and the quality suffered. With a vicious circle in bad wine as a result.

Things went so far wine-producers could only expect payment for their harvests after a solid 2 years. Many closed shop or sold their bodega's. At Gutiérrez Colosía's, they chose to wait and see: Juan-Carlos had read something about the 1882 sherry-crisis in a book, and

Gutierrez Colosia

Juan-Carlos as 'venenciador'

The naves de crianza or 'wine cathedrals'

how it was survived at the time. On the basis of that book's stimulating story, Juan Carlos decided to simply carry on. (And fortunately for us!).

Gutiérrez Colosía always had – and always will have – all that is necessary for the production of the best sherry wines. Firstly: the grapes. These solely come from Jerez Superior and vineyards with an Albariza soil. Albariza has over 60% chalk. The earth turns to a thick muddy clay when it rains; once the sun is out, it turns a smooth mirror-like crust, retaining enough water to safeguard the vines. This characteristic also reflects on the quality of the Palomino thriving here. Elsewhere in Spain, the grape gives a banal and thoroughly bland wine, the vine only being planted for the rapidity of its performance in growth and grape production. Besides the albariza-soils, there are the barros' (clay) and the 'arenas' (sand); but none produce the same quality. The best soils were entered by the Consejo Regulador in special 'pagos'. There are some 150 in all.

Gutiérrez Colosía gets most of his grapes from Balbaina Alta and Balbaina Baja, West of Jerez and Los Tercios, North of El Puerto de Santa María. The right grape is of tremendous importance in the making of a good fino.

The geographical situation and climatic conditions of the area produce quite unparalleled results. Whether or not many tried to copy the sherry: there is no equivalent! The vineyards are close to the sea, with the sun pouring down on them in summer, the temperature sometimes climbing to 40°C (these are the very best conditions for the ripening of grapes). Then there is the 'marera', the sea wind in the afternoons, bringing some freshness and moisture to the vineyards, the 'Poniente' from the Atlantic in the West and the 'Levante', a dry, warm wind from the Mediterranean.

The winds are indispensable to the right micro-climate for the wine's 'flor' when on barrel. The right conditions for its growth are not too widespread in Gutiérrez Colosía: this bodega only having its 'naves de crianza', or ripening-foyer alongside the Guadalete, and benefiting from the wind. It is the first to penetrate the Gutiérrez Colosía's barrels with their micro-organisms. Even the dry Levante carries quite a bit of moisture when around since it first sweeps over the Guadalete estuary. The flora dying away in Jerez so grows perfectly well here, all the year through, like in the Manzanilla of Sanlúcar de Barrameda.
The Fino del Puerto tastes much fruitier therefore than any sherries from Jerez, located higher up and inland. If so wanted, visitors to the bodega will be shown a weekly dating back to 1932 still mentioning 'Manzanilla del Puerto', before the Consejo Regulador decided on the present-day name.

The fruity Gutiérrez Colosía fino is sublime. But so are the intricate amontillado and the oloroso wines, both quite outstanding for the region and in their own right.

The house's winner stays the Palo Cortado however: Juan-Carlos remembers the barrels ripening from when he was a child. These prodigious wines are over 50 years old and their structure is divine. They are the very sign of the wealth contained in bodega Gutierrez Colosía.

The secret language of the solera and criadera is passed on via the marks inscribed on every vat.

Range

Gutiérrez Colosía Fino
100% Palomino
Pale yellow in colour. A very pristine nose with dabs of a well developed flor de velo, briny overtones, nuts, delicate floral touches. Light start-off but very fruity and smooth. Tasty, savoury aftertaste. The perfect balance between a biologic crianza (flor de velo) and a fruity Palomino.

Gutiérrez Colosía Amontillado
100% Palomino
Tawny golden in colour. Pristine nose with a briny bouquet and dried fruits: nuts and hazelnuts. Lovely biologic crianza holding on to sufficient fruit. Sturdy palate, the saltiness predominates. Long aftertaste. An intricate wine.

Gutiérrez Colosía Oloroso
95% Palomino, 5% Pedro Ximenez
Dark tawny colour. Red fruity nose with dabs of caramel, cocoa and chocolate. Fuller palate, woolly with lovely fruit and balance at the oxidizing stage. Long aftertaste.

Gutiérrez Colosía Palo Cortado
100% Palomino
A lovely shimmering tawny. Intense nose, pure, raisins and nuts, inviting crianza. Very sturdy and rounded palate with nice acids, intricate whole with more nuts and cocoa. Very long aftertaste. Quite unique!

Gutiérrez Colosía Moscatel Soleado
100% Moscatel
A strong tawny colour. Sweet aroma's, raisins, fig-paste, caramel and delicately woody nose. Palate starts off sweet but with sufficient acids, nicely dense, full; delightful and sweet ending with raisins in the aftertaste.

Gutiérrez Colosía, Pedro Ximenez
100% Pedro Ximenez
A gown of tawny ink. Nose of fine cocoa with whiffs of coffee, plenty of raisins, figs and dates. Full and sweet palate with the right amount of acids. Huge concentration. Sweet aftertaste.

Export

51%, mainly to Belgium, Britain, Germany, the USA and Italy.

Gutiérrez Colos
750 ml.
22% Vol. Alc.
DESDE 1838
Palo Cortado Viejísimo
Dry
gutierrez
COLOSIA
Jerez - Xérès - Sherry
Este es un Jerez Viejísimo que yo recuerdo en la
Bodega desde que era muy niño y que mi abuelo
D. José Gutiérrez Dosal cuidó con mucho esmero.
Es un 'vino de meditación' que recomiendo tomar
en algún momento especial, después de un buen día,
o para finalizar una buena comida.
Juan Carlos Gutiérrez Colosía
PRODUCE OF SPAIN
Avda. Bajamar 40
11500 El Puerto de Santa María - Cádiz - España
RE A617-CA

Bodegas Inviosa

C. La Fuente 8
Inviosa
6200 Almendralejo
Tel.: 924 67 12 35
Fax: 924 66 59 32
E-mail: inviosa@coeba.es

Marcelino Díaz

Owners: the Díaz family

Daily guided tour: Marcelino Díaz

Oenologist and agronomist: Jesús Ledesma

Surface: + 400 ha.

Production: some 1,500,000 bottles

Type: 70% red
15% white
5% rosé
10% cava

The entrance to the pioneer bodega of Extremadura

Marcelino Díaz, a pioneer and defender of Extremadura

The emperor Charles the Vth knew very well what he was doing when he picked the Extramadura to spend the last days of his life in. He had retired to the Yuste monastery, in a small village of the same name in the Sierra de Gredos. He also died there, in 1558, of an illness still prevalent today: podagra, the alcoholic variant of gout. The Extramadura wine may have been ever so slightly to blame for that.

Marceliono Diaz' Inviosa's Extramadura wines are certainly very representative of the quality of the appellation today. Marcelino is the manager and the joint-owner of bodega Inviosa. Marcelino Diaz is a 'pur sang' Extremeño; but he goes much further than most Extremeños. Extremadura has always been one of the poorest parts of Spain, a considerably demure and forlorn place in Spain's South-West; it has several municipalities, Badajoz, Merida and Cáceres. The area was always remote; even now it tends to survive almost exclusively on its agriculture. Five years ago, this somehow began to change: Extramadura enthusiastically decided to turn its weakness – or its dependency on agriculture – into a strength. The quality of its produce must be outstanding. And, nowadays, this has become obvious to all.

A number of appellations of origin were created to this effect, as a guarantee of quality. Who will not know the cerdo ibérico's 'pata negra', a terrific Spanish ham? The Extramadura DO firmly took things in hand too, providing impeccable quality controls. Another example is the valley of the Jerte with its many cherry trees. These cherries produce a liqueur the quality of which is certified by the Valle de Jerte DO. Jarandilla de la Vera's paprika powder – 'pimentón' – also has this quality label. And so on. But as far as the wine scene is concerned, the DO was the Ribera del Guadiana. It was set up in 1996.

Bodegas Inviosa, and particularly the man after the bodega, Marcelino Díaz, played a great and effective role in the creation of the DO. The estate goes back to 1931 and

Marcelino's father. Besides wine-making, there was another activity also important to him at the time: the sale of olives and olive oil. But the sectors were kept separate from the 70's onwards.

Marcelino, the youngest of the Diaz brothers, first trained as an agronomic engineer, and obtained an extra degree in oenology. After gaining some experience in a number of fields, he would definitely take the lead of the family's bodega, the 'Inviosa' (short for 'Indústrias Vinícolas del Oeste'). That was also the start of Extremadura's 'wine revolution'.

Extremadura up to now had chiefly been a 'bulk-wine' district, mainly white wines. The fact many million liters of that cheap white wine were sold to large sherry houses in the days of the dying sherry-tree, is an open secret. Much of the wine got scalded into alcohol. Not really a past and a wine-history to be terribly proud of.

Marcelino did not altogether agree with the general turn of events at the time. He liked his region and was proud of it; he was also convinced Extramadura could produce more and

The Plaza de toros of Almendralejo in the typical Moorish style of architecture is there to see for anyone who is travelling to Inviosa.

better, particularly in the wine sector. He decided to do something about things: many white vines were pulled out and replaced by red vines. Mainly Tempranillo (the traditional Spanish red wine grape), Garnacha and Graciano (also typical of Rioja).

Marcelino then went over to a selection of most of his red vines and decided to produce a crianza wine. Lar de Barros and Lar de Lares were created as trade marks; they were to effectively enter history as Extramadura's first crianza wines. Something that was not to be overlooked in an area where over 90,000 ha. is vineyard land. Not bad when one considers that Rioja e.g., an appellation and top-producer area, has some 53,000 ha. Marcelino was on the right track!

The area has six separate districts: Ribera Baja, Ribera Alta, Tierra de Barros, Matanegra, Cañamero and Montánchez. Until 1999, Inviosa wine was sold as Vino de la Tierra from the 'Tierra de Barros' sub-zone. In the year 2000 wines appeared on the market under the DO label 'Ribera del Guadiana' – the banks of the river Guadiana – or the river coming from the la Mancha heights, covering much ground in Extremadura, further flowing towards Portugal

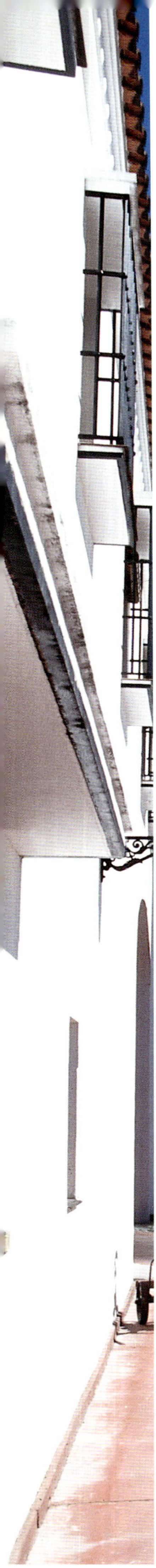

The courtyard of the bodega in Almendralejo, where the maturing of the wines takes place.

where it represents the Southern border with Spain, to finally throw itself into the Atlantic Ocean.

Inviosa has some 400 ha. vineyard surface, 225 ha. of which are covered in Tempranillo, a few ha. in Garnacha and Graciano and, for some 10 years or so, also with Cabernet Sauvignon (10 ha.). Marcelino created a different wine series for his newcomers, Cabernet Sauvignon and Chardonnay; these wines went under the name 'Lar de Oro'.

Marcelino always is ever ready to cooperate in whatever project or initiative likely to promote Extramadura abroad. This is how he organised an art competition dedicated to Salamana, in honour of that town being Cultural Capital of Europe in 2002.

Maybe one should know Inviosa wines were selected as their official 'official house wine' by another of Europe's cultural-capital in 2002, namely Bruges. This may also represent a small pat in the back to the Almendralejo region (where Extramadura is located). Many bodega's have followed Marcelino's example in the meantime and are, by now, producing very good quality wine, both red and white.

In the Almendralejo bodega, the wine is mainly layered on barrels. The reception of the grapes and the making of the wine all happen on the wine-estate in Aceuchal, a little further down the road. The Inviosa estate wine underwent a thorough change in style, and benefited greatly from technical improvements. Wine that could be considered 'a little bit country' not so very long ago is much more 'with it' nowadays. The area is also amongst Spain's first in the field of quality in relation to price.

The white wine is an excellent Macabeu with lots of fraîcheur and a super fragrant bouquet. The rosé also leapt forward as far as quality goes. The Garnacha and Tempranillo wine has quite a little body for a rosé. But the house's strong points are in its red wine varieties: the crianza de Lar de Barros, but mostly the Lar de Lares Reserva. These are the true standard references where Extramadura quality is concerned.

Another of Marcelino's darlings is the 'Bonaval' cava. The wine comes from 100% Macabeu. The DO Cava's Consejo Regulador, and that includes a number of districts in Spain, refused to recognize Extramadura 'cava land'. Cava had mainly been in Catalan hands until 1983. Marcelino once again refused to give in. The case may well go to the Spanish High Court as a result. With every due optimism however: Marcelino is producing a Cava right now; he named it DO Cava. So, Cava really can come from Extramadura!

Each year the harvest is a very special event.

Range

4 red wines

Lar de Barros, Tinto joven
100% Tempranillo.
Bright red in colour. A appealing nose of forest fruits. Lots and lots of fruit. Pleasant fraîcheur in the palate, nice fruits and well balanced acids. Sophisticated and pleasant to drink.

Lar de Barros, Crianza
85% Tempranillo, remainder Garnacha and Graciano
18 months American oak.
Bright red in colour. A very pleasant nose with red fruit, coffee, nicely dosed wood. Fairly sturdy palate to start off with: it turns lither towards the middle with appealing acids and a long aftertaste.

Lar de Lares Reserva
85% Tempranillo, remainder Garnacha and Graciano
12 months American oak.
Dark red in colour. Nice nose with black fruit, lovely touches of vanilla. Goodly rounded and fruity palate; well balanced, nice evolution. A supple and extensive aftertaste.

Lar de Oro Cabernet Sauvignon
100% Cabernet Sauvignon
10 months American oak.
Dark red in colour. Massive Cabernet nose with overtones of black fruit, mint and coffee. Black fruity palate with strong and powerful acids. All intertwining well. Beautifully bound finale.

2 white wines

Lar de Barros Macabeu
100% Macabeu
Pale yellow in colour with a lovely lustre. An exotic nose with much fraîcheur. Cool palate with dabs of melon and banana. Terrific 'passe-partout' wine. Superb with fish.

Lar de Oro Chardonnay fermentado en barrica
100% Chardonnay, 8 months
A golden gown. Typical Chardonnay nose with dabs of butter, toasted bread, vanilla, exotic fruit. Full and woolly palate with lots to spare. Powerful finale and a beautiful aftertaste.

1 rosé wine

Lar de Barros Rosado
50% Garnacha, 50% Tempranillo
A deep-pink rosé. Pleasant nose of sweets and redcurrant. Nice palate fullness with a riot of fruit. A brilliant rosé.

Méthode traditionnelle

Cava Bonaval
100% Macabeu
A neat and tidy sparkle. Spicy nose with notes of freshness. Full palate, nicely dosed. Fruit and acids are well proportioned. A pleasant bitterness in the aftertaste.

Export

55% of all production. 30% to the USA, 20% to Europe, 15% to Japan.

RESERVA 1996
Lar de Lares
RIBERA DEL GUADIANA
DENOMINACION DE ORIGEN
EMBOTELLADO POR: BODEGAS INVIOSA
AVDA. PAZ, 39 · ALMENDRALEJO · ESPAÑA
R.E. EX-06-003/0 · PRODUCT OF SPAIN
75 cl.
13% Vol.
Ribera
del Guadiana

Colophon

Text
Wim Vanleuven

Photography
Jaak Van Damme
Nicole Lepée (region Catalunya)
Humus / Graphic Group Van Damme, Oostkamp (B): pack shots

Final editing
Philippe Degryse

English translation
Belgian Translation Centre, Oostende (B)
Lena De Vlaminck, Leuven (B)

Layout & Photogravure
Humus / Graphic Group Van Damme, Oostkamp (B)

Printed by
Designdruk / Graphic Group Van Damme, Oostkamp (B)

Binding
Scheerders-Van Kerchove, Sint-Niklaas (B)

Published by
Stichting Kunstboek
Legeweg 165
B-8020 Oostkamp
Tel.: **32 50 46 19 10
Fax: ** 32 50 46 19 18
E-mail: stichting_kunstboek@ggvd.com
www.stichtingkunstboek.com

Special thanks to
Philippe Emanuelli
Olivier Fonteyne
Johan Sterckx
and
La Buena Vida
Steenweg op Mol 205
2360 Oud-Turnhout
Tel.: 014 / 45 13 03
Fax: 014 / 45 49 17
E-mail: info@labuenavida.be

ISBN: 90-5856-025-2
NUGI: 421
D/2000/6407/21